Selected Issues In Agricultural Policy Analysis With Special Reference To East Africa

Selected Issues In Agricultural Policy Analysis With Special Reference To East Africa

Tony Akaki

iUniverse, Inc.
Bloomington

Selected Issues In Agricultural Policy Analysis With Special Reference To East Africa

iUniverse books may be ordered through booksellers or by contacting:

iUniverse
1663 Liberty Drive
Bloomington, IN 47403
www.iuniverse.com
1-800-Authors (1-800-288-4677)

ISBN: 978-0-595-26248-9 (sc)
ISBN: 978-1-4620-8796-9 (sc)

Printed in the United States of America

iUniverse rev. date: 1/13/2012

Contents

ABBREVIATIONS vii

INTRODUCTION 1

METHODOLOGY 5

AGRICULTURAL POLICY ANALYSIS 7

POLICY DEMANDS 9

POLICY DECISIONS 18

POLICY OUTPUTS 37

POLICY OUTCOMES 46

POLICY IMPLICATIONS AND IMPACT: AGRICULTURAL
    MARKET REFORM 65

CONCLUSIONS 73

RECOMMENDATIONS 83

BIBLIOGRAPHY 87

ABBREVIATIONS

APPER: Africa's Priority Programme for Economic Recovery
ADMARC: Agricultural Development and Marketing Corporation
CODESRIA: Council for Development of Economic and Social Research
FAO: Food and Agriculture Organisation
GDP: Gross Domestic Product
HCPDA: Horticultural Crop Produce Development Authority
IMF: International Monetary Fund
IPC: Integrated Programme for Commodities
LDC: Less Developed Country
LIFDC: Low Income Food Deficit Countries
MPED: Manpower and Employment Department
NEP: National Extension Programme
NGO: Non Governmental Organisation
OAU: Organisation of African Unity
RNF: Rural Non Farm
SAP: Structural Adjustment Programmes
UN: United Nations
UNCTAD: United Nations Conference on Trade and Employment
UNPAAERD: United Nations of Action for African Economic Recovery and Development
NRA: National Resistance Army
BBC: British Broadcasting Corporation
SADC: Southern Africa Development Community
HIPC: Heavily Indebted Poorer Countries

ACKNOWLEDGEMENTS

Dedicated to Sofia, Haimanot, and Tsion

INTRODUCTION

The premise for this book is that broad agriculture sector policies lie at the heart of development and poverty reduction initiatives in East Africa. It is believed that the wrong agricultural policies in Eastern Africa is one of the root causes of instability and underdevelopment, most notably in Rwanda and Somalia.

It does not advance a general theory of agricultural rural development but suggest a mode of analysis in which broad sector agricultural policies can be viewed as a potentially active agent of social change and development. A study of East Africa agriculture in a country like Uganda for example, demonstrates the importance of certain considerations that are either ignored or treated as areas of only marginal concern to policy makers. This analysis will therefore attempt to answer the following:

1. What does a discussion of agriculture in Africa add to the poverty reduction concept of development in general?

2. What concept can be developed or refined by reference to past agricultural policies in East Africa?

This study provides neither the basis for valid generalisation nor grounds for invalidating established maxims. However it may contribute to comparative analysis, by uncovering relevant issues, suggesting new hypothesis and relationships, and providing evidence that is inconsistent with existing propositions.

This book does not purport to offer a comprehensive treatment of agricultural policies in East Africa, the intention is rather, to analyse certain variables and to investigate the relationship among the variables within a country specific framework.

In selecting and correlating issues, one has had to omit those which one regards of marginal relevance, in so doing one is "theorising by omission". Given the vast number of issues involved in agricultural development analysis, "theorising by omission" is unavoidable. I therefore hope my approach is not regarded as an impediment to scholarly progress.

One often finds that in writing about agricultural policy many policy-makers are concerned to answer questions about how should agricultural policy be made and implemented. In trying to do this we get preoccupied with the extent to which the policy process can be evaluated in terms of how it measures up to a "rational model" of agricultural policy having a status as a normative model.

Agricultural policy in Africa has had several "rational models" on which to base itself. During the 1960s and 1970s it was influenced by modernisation theories associated with the Chicago-based Economic Development and Cultural Change Group. A general assumption at the time was that subsistence agriculture and the mentality thought to accompany it, represents a underdeveloped mode of production which has to be overcome if Africa is to develop a "revolution of subsistence agriculture into a full commercialised system was, in the short term, the critical task facing the development community". (Gibbon, p.4).

In East Africa, Tanzania adopted a Socialist framework based on the Chinese peasant agricultural policy and traditional African values, Uganda concentrated on the smallholder farmer, whereas Kenya based its agricultural policies around large scale plantations. It is therefore clear even under the Modernisation Paradigm era a number of "rational models" emerged which, all in all, did not lead to great strides in development.

With the dawn of the 1980s a new orthodoxy emerged in the guise of structural adjustment, which came about due to the failure of the modernisation project itself. Modernisation projects were not transforming African economies. The World Bank and other donors, therefore re-defined the problem as that of lack of incentives in agriculture and targeted the state as the main hindrance, The "stages" model of development which predominated in the 1960s and 1970s was rewritten to reject the state intervention in the market place. "In practice this meant correcting administratively 'overvalued' prices (typically currency and agricultural prices) and severely reducing the size of their public sectors, especially the productive sectors of their public sectors". (Gibbon, Political Economy, p.7).

It is important therefore to note that analysis of agricultural policy-making and implementation then primarily becomes a political process. Consequently, in studying agriculture policy one has had to disrupt disciplinary boundaries and examine the social, economic and political environment in which the state operates. In so doing one raises issues of agricultural policy that may not lend themselves to neutral, value-free scientific analysis; in this regard I quote Charles Darwin, "How odd it is that anyone should not see that all observation must be for or against some view if it is to be of any service."

METHODOLOGY

More than 20 years ago, James Coleman wrote "There is no body of methods; no comprehensive methodology for the study of the impact of public policy as an aid to future policy". This now famous quote still rings true. Indeed, in the intervening decades the trend in policy analysis has become more diverse with more methodologies and conceptual frameworks being developed.

The above notwithstanding, the method of analysis used in this book is one that develops from a conceptual framework of the agricultural policy process as defined by an adapted input-output systems model of the political system. Different agricultural policy issues are then examined within this framework.

Using secondary analysis of the following major documents affecting agriculture in sub-Saharan Africa published by the World Bank:

1. Accelerated Development in sub-Saharan Africa (Berg Report)

2. From crisis to sustainable Growth

3. Towards sustained development in sub-Saharan Africa

4. Africa's Adjustment and Growth in the 1980s

a topical issue in a phenomenological sense is selected then inspected for essential elements or lack of, in light of the model and the major policy documents of the World Bank.

The World Bank's analysis and policy prescriptions for African agriculture is therefore the basis to which illuminating insights and alternatives are drawn out. In this regard a deliberate emphasis has been placed on agriculture policy making being a political process. A process that evolves through stages, with each stage more or less bounded, more or less constrained by funds and political support and other country specific factors.

Hakim (1982) defines secondary analysis as "any further analysis of an existing dataset which presents interpretations, conclusions or knowledge additional to, or different from those presented in the first report on the inquiry as a whole and it's main results". Consequently the term secondary analysis implies a reworking of data already analysed, as such, it may appear to offer little by way of originality and seem to be an unlikely method of revealing new and exacting findings.

However secondary analysis of major policy documents affecting Africa's agriculture suggests the need for a modification, if not a fundamental reframing of the traditional understanding of agricultural policy. Secondary analysis therefore serves an enlightening function of creating a new contextual understanding about agricultural issues which this study attempts to highlight and build linkages that will exist over time and educate policymakers about new developments.

AGRICULTURAL POLICY ANALYSIS

What is agricultural policy and why the current concern to focus on it, analyse it and reform it? To conceptualise the agricultural policy process I refer to a frequently used model of the functional set of categories first offered by Harold Lasswell and developed by others since.

An outline of this model is given in Figure 1. This model assumes that agriculture policy comes about in a logical path.

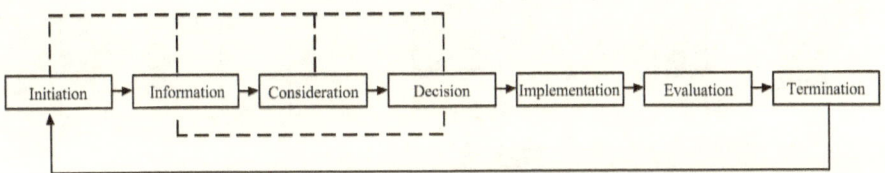

Fig. 1. Adapted Schematic presentation of process perspective on agricultural policy

(Source: Suggested by G.K. Roberts in a private communication).

This model assumes that agriculture policy comes about via a logical path. However, political behaviour rarely takes place in such an ordered way in this regard. One has had to consider the agricultural policy process in terms of an adapted input—output model of the political system derived from the work of David Easton.

Its major dimensions are indicated in Figure 2, from which it will be clear that the focus of this approach is the dynamics and processes of a national system operating in its environment. This model attempts to differentiate between:

(a) Policy demands: demands for action arising from both inside and outside the national (political) system;

7

(b) Policy decisions: authoritative rather than routine decisions by the political/national authorities;

(c) Policy outputs: what the system does—thus while agricultural exports are the most tangible output, the concept is not restricted to this;

(d) Policy outcomes (or impacts): consequences intended or unintended resulting from political action or inaction.

In this way, it becomes possible to define and explore the process of agricultural policy whilst becoming aware of the various interconnections existing within this process.

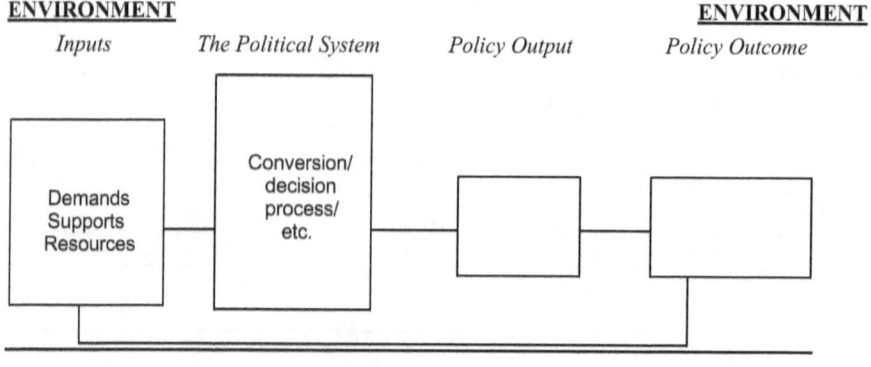

Environment: includes social, economic and political influences on inputs, policy outputs, policy outcomes, and systems variables

Figure 2: Systems Model of the Policy Process

(Source: David Easton in "A Framework for Political Analysis")

POLICY DEMANDS

Policy Supports

For policy demands to be met there must be some prerequisites for a break-through in agriculture many of which are complementary, for agricultural output and income both determine and depend upon;

1. Conditions of production: such as adequate infrastructure of roads, irrigation and inputs such as fertilisers, insecticides and farm tools, improvement of farming skills through training,

2. Levels of living: it is necessary for the farmer to have a minimum level and the right kind of education, health and nutrition,

3. Attitudes to work and life: it is necessary to increase availability of incentive goods, i.e things which the farmer and his family would work harder to get; the resistance to work in the country on the part of urban youth and technicians must be broken down,

4. Institutions: there must be a system of land tenure that encourages the farmer to produce more and be rewarded for this, rural credit must be available at low rates of interest, reform of the [state] marketing organisations so as to foster incentives for the production of both export crops and domestic food crops, for diversification often depends on more efficient marketing,

5. Policies: Policy outputs must ensure that the farmer is assured of a steady and remunerative price, technical assistance relevant to his soil, weather conditions and technology. In this case policy outputs are the policies themselves rather than the tangible outputs such as export crops.

Policy Demands of Subsistence Farming in Uganda

To reduce poverty through agricultural sector strategies in Eastern Africa entails that the policy-makers understand the role of certain food crops to African history; thereby understanding the demands for action arising from a particular mode of subsistence farming. For instance, the importance and policy demands generated by the plantain to Uganda and the Great Lakes region.

The plantain is thought to have entered the Lakes region as the early Bantu from the Ethiopian lowlands penetrated the East African uplands through the Nile-Congo divide and colonised with the banana the Great Lakes region. The banana seems to have been a decisive factor in the colonisation of the Lakes region by the proto-Interlucustine Bantu having been introduced to the East African coast by the Indonesians.

The banana is believed to have been cultivated in the Buganda region for between 1,500 and 2,000 years. McMaster (1963). The banana transformed the region from an economy based solely on fishing, hunting and collecting, to one which combined the cultivation of bananas with these extractive strategies. With the introduction of the banana, there is a subsistence shift, to plots which will remain under permanent cultivation of decades, perhaps even for generations. Consequently, access to land became the specific prerogative of small scale kin groups, and so ranking in society emerged. The introduction of banana cultivation therefore directly led to a shift from egalitarian to a rank-organised society.

Policy-makers who ignore this characteristic of subsistence plots remaining within a kin group for decades and probably for generations when formulating agricultural sector strategies of institutional building will fail. Because, once established as the principal subsistence crop, bananas were capable of producing a large and reliable calorific yield per unit of land, and per unit of labour, given the technology and the environment setting. This, in turn, has led to a well-developed rank-organised society which is present today, with kin heads serving as foci of institutionalised generosity and loci of redistribution of strategic resources.

As part of decentralisation initiatives agricultural sector programmes ideally should be administered at the local institutional level. It is believed that local programmes devised in response to local needs by local government agencies are likely to succeed. Past experience says otherwise. Apart from the critical lack of administration capacity local authorities have not always proven to be accountable to their constituencies because the local authorities also undermine the traditional rank organised institutions associated with subsistence farming, e.g. (banana).

Agricultural sector programmes in Uganda demand the considerations of the banana. Firstly, unlike grain staples that must be planted in the rainy and harvested in the dry season, bananas on the other hand can be harvested around the year and are perennials rather than annuals. Bananas have been raised on the same soil in the Buganda region of Uganda for as long as 40 years with little or no decrease in yields.

Because they yield throughout the year and are perennials, the bananas are characterised by a greater certainty and a lower labour cost than almost any other plant. Food production therefore in Buganda based on banana cultivation was so certain and so easy, in fact it could be relegated to the background of life and be left entirely to women. (Wrigley, 1957, p.71).

The exploitation of the banana as the principal vegetable staple is compatible with a social system in which a great deal of labour can be marshalled from the local community and put to work for a higher local authority. Subsistence does not suffer if men are withdrawn to take part in public works or other activities, either for themselves of for rendering service to a political authority higher than the local community.

Banana subsistence farming was conducive to colonial policy of marshalling surplus labour into cash crop farming. Consequently, within 50 years of the establishment of the British Protectorate in 1894, Ugandan agricultural development was characterised by cash crop farming of cotton and coffee for export and of labour migrating to work on farms outside their home areas in order to pay taxes, purchase education for their children at Christian schools, buy property and consumer goods with any surpluses. It is important to note that the Baganda social system around banana farming became a vital element in a colonial economy of cash-cropping by smallholder farmers assisted by immigrant traders and exporters from British India and by British-controlled marketing boards to cover the whole of the Uganda Protectorate.

Today the NRM government has recommended that Buganda's special position within Uganda should be recognised by the right of its constituents districts to combine for cultural co-operation and development under the guidance of their monarch, should majorities within those districts so decide. Needless to say, similar rights were extended to all other districts in the country. (Hansen and Twaddle, 1998, p.11).

Furthermore, the nutritional attributes of the banana make it an incomplete staple and necessitate the exploitation of other foods, this state of affairs has profound implications for the development of a particular agricultural policy that looks at an inter-regional network of exchange of higher nutritional subsistence crops and trade in general as part of a broad sector approach to agricultural development. This has led to linkages with higher value foods, most notably fish.

Fishing is an extremely important sector to the banana growing areas of East Africa, it is one of the most significant items of the peasant diet, the allocation of this fish through a redistributive hierarchy of local institutions seems to have been one important way of keeping peripheral areas under the control of a central administration. In this regard surplus male labour was important in the development of trade and exchange system linking different components of the Baganda population far away from the lake with its rich sources of protein in fish.

In studying the traditional male roles of agricultural production and development brings out issues pertinent to policy formulation today. Firstly, historians in the past used to assume that commodity production in Africa began with colonial rule. Prevailing notions took it for granted that indigenous economies were of a subsistence character and that trade began as the result of an external impact:

Arab, Indian and European. As we have seen in Buganda "exchange" was a prominent activity of the adult male population. Historians have never asked themselves how it was therefore possible for foreign traders to exchange bulk at the coast without the presence of internal traders who could first accumulate the bulk to be so traded.

State agricultural policy in the past destroyed the inter-regional markets and tied the peasant to foreign markets in which they sold industrial crops (cotton, coffee, tea). Today trade in small goods by poor farmers and traders across international boundaries have been criminalised as smuggling. Some socialist governments, for example Tanzania, put pressure on agriculture by provoking a shortage of consumer goods, particularly manufactured goods in rural areas. Fortunately for the rural populations concerned the state is not always able to suppress the intervention of private traders and parallel markets which have developed, thereby preventing total collapse of the rural sector. Agricultural policy must be linked to inter-regional trade.

Policy demands on agriculture arise not only from within as mentioned in the case of subsistence farming in Uganda, but from the environment as well which include social, economic and political influences. Probably the greatest external influence on East African agriculture is from the international financial institutions, most notably the World Bank and IMF through SAPS.

The essential ingredients of SAPs which governments are compelled to adopt as a condition for development assistance are crystallised in the World Bank Report, "Accelerated Development in Sub-Saharan Africa: An Agenda for Action", (1981, commonly known as the Berg Report). Upon its release, the Berg Report was hailed as "the New Testament for Agricultural Development" (Review of African Political Economy, [editorial], 27-8, 1983, p.186). It is important to analyse this Report to understand the policy implications to East Africa, this report called for a dramatic refocussing on agriculture in which the characterisation of the peasant farmer is one whereby he/she is being exploited by an urban alliance, growing rich and inefficient through subsidised food. Peter Gibbon sums up the re designation of the African farmer by the World Bank.

"Agriculture was no longer seen as a site of backwardness but of dynamism. This was because of its unique status as overwhelmingly the subject of private ownership. In the process the "subsistence" farmer was redesigned a "rural entrepreneur". By contrast, the industrial sector was viewed largely negatively and identified (often correctly), with state intervention, subsidisation, ineffi-ciency and general efforts at social engineering.... While LDCs still had to 'pull themselves up by their bootstraps' it was neither feasible nor desirable for them to seek to emulate the specific sectoral mix of the developed countries".

By 1989, in its second major document on sub-Saharan Africa entitled, "From Crisis to Sustainable Growth", the World Bank blames Africa for failing to develop. "Africa is simply not competitive in an increasingly competitive world". (World Bank Sub-Saharan Africa: From Crisis to Sustainable Growth: A Long Term Perspective Study. p.3). The influence of World Bank documents but particularly these two have had a fundamental impact on the environment of which agricultural policy is conducted in East Africa, consequently they are referred to frequently.

Policy Demands Created by Contract Export Farming

As mentioned earlier demands for action arise from both in side and outside the national (political) system. Inside Kenya due to the global demands for horticultural produce, farmers have abandoned growing coffee, tea and maize in favour of flowers, fruits and vegetables. Since then the industry undergone dramatic change, with exports climbing steadily since independence in 1963, when the country only used to export less than 2000 tonnes per annum.

In 1996, for example, 84824 tonnes of fresh horticulture produce were exported from Kenya, a rise of 5% in 5 years, according to the Nairobi-based Horticultural Crop Produce Development Authorities (HCPDA). This figure accounts for 10% of the country's export earnings making it the third most important agricultural export after tea and coffee. "By the year 2000 Kenya's export of fresh horticultural produce are expected to surpass the 100000 tonne mark", the HCPDA predicts. This put Kenya second only to the World's largest flower exporters, Israel and Colombia.

Outside the national political system the IMF and World Bank have influenced agricultural policy. The solutions they proposed for Africa's economic recovery depended on using an agriculturally based export-oriented growth strategy. The World Bank stated "the agriculture-based and export-orientated development stategy suggested for the 1980s is an essntial beginning to a process of long-term transformation, a prelude to industialization." (Accelerated Development, p6 1981)

The Berg Report further stated "The projected rate of growth of trade in Africa's main exports is 1ower than that of overall world trade. This dependence on exports of slowly growing primary products is a disadvantage, but exports can be diversified and Africa's share of world trade in most commodities could be increased with relatively small effects on prices." (Accelerated Development, p23, 1981)

The report's recommendation to diversify is based on the Law of comparative advantage which holds that "a country [should] produce those things which it can best produce as compared with other countries and second,[it must continue] producing them with the least use of limited resources" (Accelerated Development, p24, 1981)

The policy implications of this export-growth strategy for Africa according to the World Bank is that higher producer prices for exports will not only induce the "market peasant" to grow these crops, they will form the basis of improved and more efficient production of food as well. The World Bank dismisses the argument that a concentration on export crops occurs at the expense of food crops, the report argues that this is not necessarily a bad thing. "Even if it could be demonstated that export increases have come at the expense of food production, the conclusion would not necessarily follow that a strategy of self reliance requires a substitution of food production for exports. Most African countries have distinct comparative advantage in export crop production" (accelerated Development, p63-4)

The assumption of the World Bank is that self-reliance in food can best be attained by exporting in which a country enjoys a comparative advantage and importing food that is cheaper than it would cost to produce locally. However in Kenya cut flowers are now one of the country's most lucrative agricultural export, with growth forecast at 10% per year over the next 5 years. In the 1990s farmers were abandoning the farming of food crops like maize and beans in favour of horticultural produce at a time when the El Nino phenomenon and drought had led to food insecurity.

According to a new report, the promotion of cash crops and commercialisation of small holder agriculture in Kenya has contributed to poverty and food insecurity. The report which is opposed to the World Bank position is titled "The Role of Commercialisation in Food Productivity: The Case of Kenya" jointly compiled by the Kenya Tegemeo Institute/Egerton University, the Kenya Agriculture Research Institute and Michigan State University warns that the industry will increase the gap between the rich and the poor. This has created new policy demands regarding food security and poverty reduction.

In line with the World Bank view of development of cash crops 12% of all sub-Saharan peasant farmers were growing sugar, tea, tobacco, fresh fruit and vegetables under contract with either state or private suppliers for the international market. Between them they accounted for 17% of the total produced by all farms and for 30% of everything marketed. (Watts, 1970, p152)

Agricultural contracts in East Africa and most notably in Kenya are arranged in three ways. In one, large suppliers offer direct contracts to small farmers, but negotiate the terms through their own organisations either with the State or with some local institutions; in another, small peasants are offered contracts either by local or foreign merchants. The commonest system is one operated by large processing and shipping organisations, often owned by the State which give limited contracts, almost invariably of one year in duration, to innumerable small peasant growers. These contracts determine what is to be grown, the methods to be used and the price to be paid; those who issue them take absolute title of the crop.

The World Bank has been at the forefront of urging the practice of contract farming as a "new agricultural policy" in tandem with it's SAPs. The contract farming system benefits a small coterie which may well satisfy the Bretton Woods institutions and the trickle down theorists. But probably the most important policy demand to come out of contract farming lies in the extent to which it encourages inter and intra-communal competition for productive land, and to which it engenders clientalistic politics.

Due to an increase in plantation and contract farming combined with drought, domestic food production in Kenya fell between 1979 and 1993 by an average of 0.4% (World *Bank, 1995).* This forced the Kenyan government to import substantial quantities of cereals, from 1980 to 1993, annual cereal imports increased from 387,000 metic tonnes to 569,000 metric tonnes. Simultaneously, the value added to agriculture declined from just over US$2 billion to under US$1.4 billion. This too can partly be attributed to contract farming.

It is important to note here, like in so many other scenarios regarding agricultural policy a number of variables are responsible for Kenya importing cereals from 1980 to 1993 which cannot be attributed to contracting farming alone. The National Food Policy paper stated the unprecedented 4% rate of growth of population and a smallholder credit repayment rate of 20%. At the time the message of the National Food Policy was clear: Kenya has a major food production constraint that cannot be overcome except through large investments in agricultural research, irrigation and land reclamation throughout the 1980s and 1990s. But one wonders why the National Food paper paid lip service to population growth.

Population-Environment-Poverty Nexus

Population growth has been one of the problematic demands on African agriculture since the 1970s. Rapid population growth or overpopulation has led to overgrazing, overcultivation and deforestation. The 1991 World Development Report cites overpopulation as the root cause of environmental degradation. This argument is based on what is described as the population-environment-poverty nexus. Reference to this phenomenon suggests the remergence of neo-Malthusian arguments of the 1970s based on the need for population controls as the answer to agricultural development.

But managing populations through a superficial and narrowly technical neo-Malthusianism way can sometimes produce an opposite reaction to the one sought. A good example of this is in the case of Islamic countries whereby the new population reducing technologies were seen as methods by which the West aimed to perpetuate its dominance. The world population conference held in Cairo in 1994 revealed harsh reactions to crude technocratic approach to population control. Yet the pressures of overpopulation through systems of shifting agricultural production, added to drought, continue their work of deforestation, soil erosion and desertification. This has led to increased rural-urban migration, which in turn further increases a country's food deficit and adds to the social inequalities and political instability. It is therfore imperative that population policies attempt to affect, the size, structure or geographic distribution of population. In practice however, it may be difficult to make a clear distinction between those measures that influence population growth deliberately—that is directly and those that influence it indirectly through the side effects of other agricultural/public policies.

POLICY DECISIONS

Policy Decisions: Education and Agricultural Productivity

In 1992–93, the poorest half of the population of Uganda received over 4/5 of their incomes from agriculture (World Bank), therefore as education complements capital and substitutes for labour, the returns to schooling in Uganda and other East African countries should cover returns in the agricultural sector.

Agricultural productivity is influenced through cognitive and non-cognitive effects of education. Cognitive schooling aims to develop general skills such as numeracy, literacy and the transmission of specific knowledge. Some African countries in a bid to boost productivity have initiated policy decisions to teach specific agricultural knowledge in schools without much success, more weight is still placed on the formation of general skills.

Non-cognitive effects of schooling have the effect of changing people's attitudes and practices, it is important to point out here that non-cognitive effects are usually discussed in the context of industry rather than agriculture, with sociologists noting the similarity between the classroom and the factory floor. Nevertheless non-cognitive effects of education on agriculture opens up a number of possibilities.

In analysing agricultural policy it is important to estimate the effect of education on agricultural productivity~ Africa. TABLE 1 summarizes the microeconometric estimates of the effect of education on agricultural productivity in East Africa compiled by Simon Appleton (University of Oxford) and Arsene Balihuta (Makerere University).

These estimates may have been overlooked in agricultural policy decisions because they are not published in main stream journals furthermore they come from studies which are not focused specifically in the impact of the education curriculum on agriculture. Given the importance of the agricultural sector to many East African countries it is imperative that agricultural policy matters create linkages with other sectors in order to formulate accurate data to which future policy decisions can be based. It is also important to note that education variables are usually defined only by reference to the education of the household head and that the dependent variable is commonly either the output of a single crop or total agricultural output. Furthermore researchers commonly estimate production functions, with land, labour and capital as additional determinants of output.

Table 1. Existing studies on education and agricultural productivity in Africa

Area & study	Data	Dependent variable	Estimated effect of farmer education variable(s)	Other comments
Kenya 1. Kenya (Hopcraft 1974)	674 small farms surveyed in 1969–70	Maize production	Negative and sometimes significant	
		Combined crop and livestock production	Essentially zero	
2. Kenya Vihiga (Moock, 1981)	101 male-headed farms in Vihiga district surveyed 1971–72	Maize production per acre	1-3 yrs schooling significantly negative more than 4 years insignificant (relative to no education)	
3. Kenya (Bigsten, 1984)	Integrated Rural Survey 1: 1613 farms surveyed in 1974–75	Crop production	1-4 years schooling significantly positive further schooling insignificant and positive Mixed and insignificant results Positive but insignificant	Sizeable effect even though seldom significant eg those with some secondary schooling are predicted to have 39% higher combined output ceteris paribus
		Livestock production		
		Combined crop and livestock production		

Table 1. Existing studies on education and agricultural productivity in Africa (Continued)

Area & study	Data	Dependent variable	Estimated effect of farmer education variable(s)	Other comments
4. Kenya (Bevan et al, 1989)	Integrated Rural Survey 5 (IRS 5): 783 households surveyed in 1982. Subsamples used in analysis	Coffee production Hybrid maize production	Positive but insignificant Positive but insignificant	Fairly largr magnitudes: some primary education raises coffee output by 21%;maize by 28%
5. Kenya (Aguilar and Bigsten, 1994)	IRS 5: subsample of 693 households	Crop production	Positive and insignificant in Central and coffee growing areas: Negative significant in Nyanza and negative insignificant in non-coffee growing areas	Definition of education as a 5 level categorical variable unclear and may not be best specification empirically
6. Kenya (Husbands et al., forthcoming)	103 households in a village in Muranga district in 1991–92	Combined crop and livestock production	Without controls for cognitive skills and reasoning ability, schooling is insignificant	
Other countries Tanzania (Collier et al, 1986)	540 households surveyed in 20 villages in 1980	Crop production Livestock production	Positive, significant Positive, insignificant	Effect of categorical education on crop production hard to interpret; authors cite 27% effect of complete primary schooling

Table 1. Existing studies on education and agricultural productivity in Africa (Continued)

Area & study	Data	Dependent variable	Estimated effect of farmer education variable(s)	Other comments
8. Tanzania (Pinckney & Kimuyu, 1995)	95 households surveyed in one village Kiliman-garo region, 1991–92	Combined crop and livestock production	Without controls for cognitive skills and reasoning ability, 4 or more years of primary schooling have a positive, significant effect	
9. Burkina Faso (Ram & Singh 1988)	51 households in 7 villages the Mossi plateau	Crop production minus cost of purchased inputs	School years of all farmworkers positive, significant with 7% rate of return	Schooling of house-hold head not significant as educational variable
10. Cote d'Ivoire (Gurgand, 1993)	686 households surveyed in 1985 Living Standards Survey	Combined crop and livestock production	Education variables neither insignificant or negative	No controls for labour inputs
11. Ethiopia (Aredo et al., 1995)	277 households in Arssi & Sina-Debre-Sina provinces surveyed in 1989–91	Combined crop and livestock production	Numeracy had positive but insignificant effect on farm efficiency	Education variables not entered

**Table 1. Existing studies on education and agricultural productivity in
Africa (Continued)**

Area & study	Data	Dependent variable	Estimated effect of farmer education variable(s)	Other comments
12. Ethiopia (Cropenstedt & Demeke, 1995)	149 farms in Arssi province surveyed in 1989–91	Wheat and barley production	Numeracy had positive significant effect on farm efficiency	Education variables not entered
13. Uganda (Bigsten & Kayizzi-Mugerwa, 1995)	198 farms in rural Masaka district surveyed in 1990	Agricultural production	Variables for some primary-secondary and post-secondary education of house-hold head all insignificant	Coefficients on education not reported but in Bigsten & Kayizzi-Mugerwa (1996) are of non-negligible size.

Source: Appleton and Balihuta, (Makerere University)

In East Africa the policy implications regarding returns to general education (Schooling) vis-a-vis agriculture are important in that, past agricultural policymakers concentrated on returns to farmer education only (e.g extension) without considering the general education the farmer and his community had received. In this regard it is important for policymakers to note that farmer education is enhanced by schooling in general. In analysing agricultural policy it is important to estimate the returns of both. However the distinction between the two is getting blurred in that specific agricultural knowledge characteristic of extension activities is being incorporated within the general primary and secondary school curricula.

In summarizing the studies in TABLE 1 a number of reasons were suggested for the lack of significance of education. In a few cases the samples were to small. More generally, agricultural production is likely to be measured with considerable error. Nevertheless education appears to raise household consumption other things being constant, amongst the poor and non-poor. Given the high dependence of the poor on agriculture for their incomes as noted earlier, this suggests that education may raise agricultural productivity.

Education and Subsistence Farming Systems in Uganda

As mentioned earlier during the discussion concerning the plantain, policymakers must understand the role of certain food crops thereby understanding the demands for action arising from a particular mode of subsistence farming. In this regard it is important to note that there are a number of very different agro-ecological zones within Uganda and the scope of policy decisions and hence responses in each of these may vary. Consequently education may be important in zones and not in others.

TABLE 2 gives some summary information on the characteristics of farms surveyed by Simon Appleton and Arsene Balihuta using Uganda's first nationally reprsentative household survey in each of the 5 farming systems identified by Parsons (1970)

The 5 Farming Systems in Uganda

(1) The banana-coffee system: it is the largest and covers most of the central area bounded between Lakes Victoria, Albert and Kyoga.

(2) Teso: The principal crops grown in the second systems are sweet potatoes, millet, sorghum and groundnuts, it covers the 3 districts of Kumi, Soroti and Pallisa.

(3) Northern: this system is characterised by relatively low rainfall; and sesame accounting for a substantial proportion of agricultural revenue. In some areas of this system the people rely on communal labour for cultivation.

(4) Montane: These grow similar crops to the banana and coffee system, but have a higher altitude and greater pop~ulation density. (also found in Rwanda)

(5) Karamoja: Pastoral system covering two districts in the North East, these areas grow Sorghum and Maize. The area has very few educated farm workers (averaging only 1 year of primary schooling per farm compared with 5 years elsewhere).

Table 2 Farming systems in Uganda

Variables	*Banana-coffee*	*Teso*	*Northern*	*Montane*	*Karamoja*
Mean characteristics					
Log agricultural output	12.25	11.81	11.97	12.35	10.81
Log labour	5.11	5.16	5.16	5.19	4.94
Log land	3.18	3.22	3.39	2.97	3.06
Log purchased inputs	10.85	11.21	11.17	10.91	10.92
Log capital	8.91	8.84	9.02	8.84	8.49
Total years of primary schooling of farm workers	5.62	5.47	5.74	5.44	1.03
Percentage of revenue from:					
Maize	8	3	5	7	24
Sorghum	1	11	8	3	43
Millet	5	14	9	4	10
Rice	0	4	0	0	0
Other grains	0	0	0	0	3
Matooke	20	2	1	36	0
Cassava	21	6	18	8	0
Sweet potatoes	12	33	13	11	3
Other tubers	1	0	0	4	0
Beans	11	1	7	13	2
Peas	0	1	3	0	3
Groundnuts	3	9	9	0	2
Sim-sim	0	1	12	0	0

Table 2 Farming systems in Uganda (Continued)

Variables	Banana-coffee	Teso	Northern	Montane	Karamoja
Other pulses/ nuts	0	1	1	0	1
Fruits	3	1	1	2	0
Vegetables	1	1	2	1	1
Cotton	1	3	2	0	0
Coffee	6	0	0	3	0
Other cash crops	0	0	1	0	3
Cobb-Douglas Production Functions[1:]					
Intercept	6.86(30.0)***	7.43(11.3)***	7.34(19.6)***	7.16(17.3)***	5.86(5.0)***
Log labour	0.17(4.7)***	0.14(1.3)	-0.04(0.8)	0.25(4.1)***	0.25(1.3)
Log land	0.36(15.8)***	0.36(4.9)***	0.33(9.4)***	0.39(9.9)***	0.45(2.6)**
Log capital	0.08(5.1)***	0.121(2.3)*	0.19(7.2)***	0.08(3.0)***	0.14(1.4)
Log purchased inputs	0.23(16.6)***	0.12(3.1)***	0.17(8.4)***	0.18(7.7)***	0.10(1.3)
Total years of primary school-ing of farm workers	0.011(3.4)***	0.03(3.2)***	0.012(2.5)**	0.006(1.2)	-0.009(-0.2)
Adjusted R-squared	0.33	0.30	0.28	0.27	0.26
Number of observations	2355	382	1091	972	77

[1] Estimated coefficients (T-ratios in brackets)
Source: Appleton and Balihuta

To see how the impact of education differs across farming systems they estimated separate production functions for each system. (Table2). They also used the Cobb-Douglas rather than the translog functional form and included total years of primary schooling of the farm workers as the only measure of education. The only other variables included were the 4 factors of production (land, labour, purchased inputs and capital).

As TABLE 2 shows Appleton and Balihuta have presented original results for Uganda that show that the estimated effect of education is significant and exactly in line with the developing country mean calculated by Lockheed et al.: 4 years of primary schooling appears to raise production by 7%. These results should re enforce policymakers and hence policy decisions towards an improved education system which may well benefit those in the agricultural sector, who include the poorest people in the country.

Positive externalities may also be reaped from education, in that if education changes a farmer's practices, these may be easily seen and copied by neighbouring farmers. Such spillovers are particularly important in the case for public funding of education, these externalities from primary education do provide a simple prima facie case for public subsidy.

Consequently, if the goals of agricultural policy are to be achieved through universal education, there is no real alternative to increased public investment. But under SAPs in many African countries, cutbacks in education expenditure and the imposition of higher fees on parents have led to the curtailment of enrolments

Policy Decisions: The issue of Rural Non-Farm Income

The issue of RNF income development as a policy of an agricultural strategy has become an important consideration among policy makers. In the past (1960s) agricultural policy was viewed on the basis of the single-minded pursuit of the goal of increased output. Today policy decisions should be directed at achieving multiple objectives.

The following objectives quoted from (Johnson 1972) seem to be especially relevant to agricultural policy decisions in the broad sense:

(1) Contributing to the overall rate of economic growth and the process of structural transformation,

(2) Achieving a satisfactory rate of increase in farm output at minimum cost by encouraging sequences of innovations which exploit the possibilities for technical change most appropriate to a country's factor endowments.

(3) Achieving a broadly based improvement in the welfare of the rural population, and

(4) Facilitating the process of social modernization (including the extension and improvement of rural education, and the strengthening of entrepreneurial capacities) by encouraging widespread attitudinal andbehavioural changes among farm households.

Johnson (1972) believed that it is "useful to assess the 'total efficiency' of alternative agricultural stategies in terms of their success in achieving those four objectives". His concept of total efficiency, however is difficult to define, but must be confronted by policy makers in deciding whether a country's agricultural strategy is efficient in this broad sense, by the trade-off between the goal of increased output and other objectives likely to be minimised.

But over the past 30 years the agriculture sector has changed. In sub-Saharan Africa there has been a pronounced shrinkage in this sector from 79% of the labour force in 1965 to 67% in 1990–92 (TABLE3). This relative decrease in agricultural employment has been mirrored by a similar decline in the proportion of the population resident in rural areas, estimated at 85% in 1960 and 69% in 1992 for the whole of sub-Saharan Africa. It is therefore clear to see that a sizeable proportion of the African population no longer work primarily as rural farmers.

Furthermore, market liberalization and economic crisis have combined to create a stimulus for people to pursue any combination of agricultural/non-agricultural activities regardless of rural or urban location.

Table 3 Share of non-farm income and employment in total rural income and employment

Regions and subregions	Non-farm income share		Non-farm employment share		Average per caput GNP2, 1995 ($)
	Mean[3] (%)	Coefficient of variation	Mean[3] (%)	Coefficient of variation	
AFRICA	42	0.45	-	-	726
East & southern Africa	45	0.47	-	-	932
West Africa	36	0.36	-	-	313
ASIA	32	0.33	44	0.32	1847
East Asia	35	0.19	44	0.29	2889
South Asia	29	0.52	43	0.40	388
LATIN AMERICA	40	0.20	25	0.33	2499

1. The data given are regional averages of country cases. The income shares represent the share of non-farm income in the total income of households that are mainly farm households (including the rural landless). The employment shares represent the share of households in the rural population (in both rural areas and small rural towns) for which non-farm activity is the primary occupation.

2. Average per caput GNP is calculated as the simple average over the countries covered by the case studies. It is based on estimates from World Bank, 1997. World Development Report 1997. Washington DC.

3. The mean refers to the mean over the case studies considered for each region and subregion.

Source: FAO

The rural-urban divide has become extremely hazy. Non-agricultural activities on the part of rural households have also proliferated. The importance of this RNF activity to policy making in Africa cannot be overstated when compared across developing country regions—as seen in (TABLE4); which summarizes data on the shares of non-farm income and employment in total rural income and employment drawn from studies from the 1970s to the 1990s in Africa, Asia and Latin Amenca.

It is clear that average non-farm income shares are higher in Africa (42%) and Latin America (40%) than in Asia (32%), these findings are important to the decision taking process in that they show that non-farm income is a significant part of total income and hence important for purchasing power and food secu-rity. Interestingly one would expect the relative importance of non-farm income to be greater in regions with higher levels of GNP per capita as richer regions tend to have better infrastructure and stonger agricultural sectors which induce RNF development.

However, as Africa is placed first in the ranking this suggests to policymakers that diversification incentives have an important role to play. That is although African households are poorer than those in other regions, the incentive to diversify their incomes is strong (owing to low farm incomes, risks, etc.) This is a turn about to the widely held view that sees African peasants as being inclined towards rural income diversification. Nevertheless, within individual regions, the richer coun-tries and sub regions do tend to show higher shares and levels of RNF income.

As previously mentioned policymakers cannot afford to ignore the influence of subsistence farming systems or the agroclimatic conditions that favour certain crops like the plantain in the Buganda region in Uganda. The nature and perfor-mance of local agriculture can affect the development of the RNF sector in a par-ticular System. Generally speaking where the agroclimate is poor (e.g karamoja in Uganda), households tend to earn more from migration than from local non-farm activity. The reverse holds for favourable agroclimates such as in Baganda with it's dynamic agriculture-households tend to earn most non-farm income locally, mainly in activity generated by production or expenditure linkages with the agricultural sector.

With this in mind policy decisions regarding agricultural policy and RNF activity will have to take into account:

—the local price of the agricultural product and it's effects on the profitability of downstream processing (e.g price of inputs)

—the output price of food and it's general effect on the RNF sector through it's impact on wages

—the effect of a change in the agricultural wage has on the non-farm wage. Indeed, an increase in the agricultural wage may spread to the non-agricultural sector and cause the unskilled non-farm wage to increase.

—the factor bias of agricultural technology (labour-intensive or capital intensive) and the seasonality of farm labour requirements which both influence the supply of labour to RNF employment

—the composition of agricultural output and ifs effects on non-farm opportunities. The crop variety and harvest timing affect RNF oportunities through their effects on processing. There tends to be a correlation between agricultural diversification (away from starchy staples) and income diversification into non-farm activities. As agriculture diversifies into fishing, livestock products, fruit and vegetables, opportunities for value added (agroprocessing) increase. Such diversification is generally induced by increasing incomes, which raise demand for foods other than starchy staples.

—Education is an important factor vis a vis a more"egalitarian" income distribution. Equitable access to education leads to access to urban wage employment and agricultural innovations leads to higher productivity. Investments generated with off farm and migration income (of which education is a strong determinant) causes productivity increases for poor and rich households alike, thereby enhancing the equalizing effects of access to off farm employment.

Selected Issues In Agricultural Policy Analysis With Special Reference To East Africa

Table 4 Statistical indices of African de-agrarianisation 1960–62

Country	Real GDP			Urban PGR				Rural Population		% of Labour force in					
	Population million	Per capita US $	Annual PGR* %	%	%	%		% of total		Agriculture		Industry		Services	
	19 92	19 91	60-92	60-92	70-80	80-92	change	19 60	19 92	19 65	90-92	19 65	90-92	19 65	90-92
Angola	9.9	1000	2.3	5.9				90	73	79	73	8	10	13	17
Benin	4.9	1500	2.5	7.4	8.5	5.2	-3.3	91	60	83	70	5	7	12	23
Botswana	1.3	4690	3.2	13.5	10.0	8.8	-1.2	98	73	88	28	4	11	8	61
Burkina Faso	9.5	666	2.4	4.6	6.4	8.7	2.3	95	83	90	87	3	4	7	9
Burundi	5.8	640	2.2	5.5	7.7	5.1	-2.6	98	94	94	92	2	2	3	8
Cameroon	12.2	2400	2.6	6.5	7.5	5.4	-2.1	86	58	87	79	4	7	9	14
Cape Verde	0.4	1360	2.1	4.1				84	70		31		6		63
C.A.R.	3.2	641	2.3	3.6	4.7	4.7	0.0	77	52	88	81	3	3	9	16
Chad	5.9	447	2.1	7.1	7.8	6.8	-1.0	93	66	92	83	3	5	5	12
Comoros	0.6	469	3.2	6.8				90	71		83		6		11
Congo	2.4	2800	2.8	3.6	3.7	4.5	0.8	68	58	66	62	11	12	23	26
Cote d'Ivoire	12.9	1510	3.9	6.5	7.4	4.7	-2.7	81	58	80	65	5	8	15	27
Djibouti	0.5	1000	5.7	7.3				50	14						
Equatorial Guinea	0.4	700	1.2	1.5				75	71		77		2		21
Ethiopia	53.1	370	2.5	4.8	4.8	4.8	0.0	94	87	86	88	5	2	9	10
Gabon	1.2	3498	3.0	6.3	8.3	5.8	-2.5	83	53		75		11		14
Gambia	0.09	763	3.0	5.2				87	76		84		7		9
Ghana	16.0	930	2.7	3.9	2.9	4.3	1.4	77	65	61	59	15	11	24	30
Guinea	6.1	500	2.1	5.3	4.8	5.8	1.0	90	73	87	78	6	1	7	21

Guinea Bissau	1.0	747	2.0	3.2	5.8	3.8	-2.0	86	80		82		4		14
Kenya	25.3	1350	3.5	7.7	8.5	7.7	-0.8	93	75	86	81	5	7	9	12
Lesotho	1.8	1500	2.4	8.6	6.9	6.7	-0.2	97	79	91	23	3	33	6	44
Liberia	2.8	850	3.1	6.2				81	53	79	75	10	9	11	16
Madagascar	12.9	710	2.8	5.6	5.3	5.7	0.4	89	75	85	81	4	6	11	13
Malawi	10.3	800	3.4	6.5	7.5	6.1	-1.4	96	88	92	87	3	5	5	8
Mali	9.8	480	2.6	4.4	4.8	5.2	0.4	89	75	91	85	1	2	8	13
Mauretania	2.1	962	2.4	9.8	10.4	7.2	-3.2	94	50	89	69	3	9	8	22
Mozambique	15.1	921	2.2	9.5	11.5	9.9	-1.6	96	70	87	85	6	7	7	8
Namibia	1.5	2381	2.8	4.8	4.9	5.1	-0.2	85	71		43		22		35
Niger	8.3	542	3.2	7.4	7.5	7.3	-0.2	94	81	95	85	1	3	4	12
Nigeria	115.9	1360	2.7	6.3	6.1	5.7	-0.4	86	63	72	48	10	7	18	45
Rwanda	7.5	680	3.2	7.4	7.5	3.8	-3.7	98	94	95	90	2	2	3	8
Sao Tome	0.1	600	2.1						74						
Senegal	7.8	1680	2.8	3.5	3.7	4.0	0.3	68	59	83	81	6	6	11	13
Seychelles	0.1	36983	1.7												
Sierra Leone	4.4	1020	2.1	5.2	5.2	5.2	0.0	87	69	78	70	11	14	11	16
Somalia	9.3	759	2.8	5.8	3.8	4.0	0.2	83	65	81	76	6	8	13	16
South Africa	13.9	3885	2.6	3.2	2.8	2.8	0.0	53	50	32	13	30	25	38	62
Sudan	26.7	1162	2.8	5.4	5.0	4.1	-0.9	90	77	81	72	5	5	14	23
Swaziland	0.8	2506	2.8	10.5				96	72		74		9		17
Tanzania	27.9	570	3.2	10.3	11.4	6.6	-4.8	95	78	91	85	3	5	6	10
Togo	3.8	738	2.9	6.2	8.6	5.5	-3.1	90	71	78	65	9	6	13	29
Uganda	18.7	1036	3.3	6.1	3.7	5.0	1.3	95	88	91	86	3	4	6	10
Zaire	40.0	469	3.0	4.8				78	71	82	71	9	13	9	16
Zambia	8.6	1010	3.2	7.1	5.9	3.8	-2.1	83	58	79	38	8	8	13	54

Zimbabwe	10.6	21 60	3.2	5.9	5.8	5.9	0.1	87	70	79	71	8	8	13	21
Sub-Saharan Africa	56 0.2	13 14.02 2	2.8	5.2	6.3	5.4	- 0.9	85	69	79	67	8	8	13	25
Least dev'd countries	54 0.0	23 7	2.5	5.3				92	79	83	73	6	8	11	19
Developing countries	42 40.0 0	77 0	2.3	4.0	3.7	3.7	0.0	78	65	72	58	11	15	17	27
Industrial countries	12 10.0 7	17 01	0.8	1.4				39	27	22	9	37	33	41	58
World	54 50.0 0	38 36	1.8	2.9	2.6	2.8	0.2	66	56	57	43	19	21	24	36

Sources: UNDP, Human Development Report 1994; World Bank, World Development Report 1994 PGR—population growth rate

Policy decisions: Issues regarding RNF Activity

In order to achieve an efficient use of resources throughout a given economy, African national governments have got to design general macroeconomic policies that enhance the development of RNF activities. The beneficial effect of these policies with regard to improved resource allocation should extend to the rural areas, particuarly to the extent that they eliminate the urban bias frequently found in African economic policies.

However the effects of these macro economic policies while creating opportunities for RNF activity can also remove the protection previously enjoyed by the RNF sector and expose certain RNF subsectors to competition from urban-based enterprises and imports. This is particularly true in countries undertaking SAP as this means the redction if not the elimination of state involvement in the rural productive and marketing infrastructure.

Rural infrastructure investment policies by the state can create linkages between the RNF sector and agriculture thus creating RNF multipliers from the growth of agriculture. This investment includes provision of hard infrastructure (e.g roads, electrification) and soft infrastructure (e.g banking systems, market information systems) as a Means of reducing the transaction costs for business in rural areas.

As the RNF sector is linked to agriculture in most of East Africa apart from areas with adverse agroclimatic. It is important that sector specific policies in general and agriculture policies in particular do not neglect RNF development. Sector-specific policies should be designed within the political system to identify promising subsectors and then systematically address the constraints to incentives and capacity for development—ranging from the participation of small and medium scale farmers, small and medium-sized agro-industrial development and/or linkages with larger agro-industrial companies.

Probably the biggest issue pertaining to RNF activity and the State, is that this sector has fallen into an "institutional vacuum" as it neither belongs within the domain of Agricultural ministries, with their mandate related to farming nor to industry ministries which commonly focus on large-scale, formal sector companies.

Policy makers have to take the decision to establish a system perspective that links the agricultural and RNF sectorial domains. This will lead to close cooperation in policy and programme formulation and implementation between agriculture and

other ministries (e.g commerce, industry, natural resources, etc.) with respect to
rural development in general and RNF sector specifically.

POLICY OUTPUTS

This chapter highlights what the state or the political system does. An increase in agricultural exports is frequently the goal often pursued, but in this case agricultural output is not restricated to this. The policy outputs of agriculture are rooted in increasing the level of per capita of a country to a level that can enhance the agricultural sector's contribution to economic development and food security. The above notwithstanding, agricultural production in sub-Saharan Africa fell by 1% in 1997, implying a 4% fall in per capita terms thus interrupting a 4 year period of expansion in per caput agricultural output. This fall in production is directly attributed to the effects of the El Nino weather phenomeon, which led to the number of countries facing food emergencies to rise from 29 in mid-1997 to 36 in mid-1998.

In East Africa recent drought followed by floods and civil strife in a few countries has led to food shortages. Somalia's food supply situation is likely to remain after the worst floods in decades sharply reduced the 1997/98 secondary crops. Loss of livestock and an outbreak of animal disease like foot and mouth have also resulted.

Flooding in Eastern Kenya has led to the population relying on food assistance, which is also required for some 400,000 displaced people in the northern areas affected by continuing insurgency. Food aid is also needed by more than 5 million vulnerable Ethiopians, including those affected by a poor 1997 harvest. Two successive reduced cereal harvests in Eritrea in 1998 led to a sharp rise in food prices. Civil strife in Sudan has also led to a critical food situation and assistance is now required for some 2.4 million people.

The secondary 1997/98 crop in parts of Tanzania was reduced by heavy rains and floods leading to food difficulties. Rwanda and Burundi have also not fared well, owing to a reduced 1998 first-season harvest and insecurity in the former and a decline in the 1998 first season foodcrop production in the latter.

Managing Cyclical Drought: The Kenyan Experience.

Kenya has shown that subsistence crisises in Africa need not precipitate political disorder as was the case in Ethiopia and Somalia; rather they can and have been used to consolidate political power. The vast bulk of Kenyan grain is produced in Rift Valley, Nyanza and Western provinces and to moniter food supplies the Kenyan government maintains an official bureaucracy (Maize Board) to guarantee food security.

The Board maintains a series of depots and purchasing centres around Kenya concentrated obviously in the maize growing provinces. Over 805 of the storage facilities of the Board lie on rail sidings in the above provinces. The government also maintains a national administration called the Provincial Administration whose job is to preserve order through the civilian bureaucracy, the police and other internal security forces.

During the food security crisis of 1979–80 and 1984–85, the 2 bureaucracies merged. The Provincial Administration superintended, as a matter of national security, the operations of the maize Board and directed the procurement, storage and distribution of the nation's food reserves. Under the direction of the Provincial Administration, the Board's officers in Nairobi asserted their "ownership" of the stocks of grain held in it's depots in the producing regions

Not only did the Kenyan bureaucracy seize physical contol of the grain stocks in the producing regions, it also moved them from storage facilities in the farm lands to storage depots in the consuming areas. To initiate this "strategic transfer" of maize it deployed trucks and railway wagons to transport grain from depots in the growing provinces to storage houses of the Board and the maize milling companies in Nakuru Kisumu, Mombasa and Nairobi.

The government sought not only to control and direct supplies already in it's possession; it also sought to speed up the flow of grain from farm producers into it's marketing facilities. To achieve this, it built a network of local buying centres and offered farmers the "into depot" price for grain delivered to these centres. The benefit to the farmer was a rise in the price offered by the government, as the government now paid for the cost of transportation to it's railway depots.

A common theme throughout both food crises was the virtual "nationalisation" of the surpluses generated in the maize growing districts, these acts of command and control are a fundamental characteristic of maize marketing in Kenya. The

World Bank on the otherhand advocates that the market and not the state should allocate resources. (Accelerated Development, p.43 1981). But it recognises that the "devolution of marketing functions to private enterprise may be more difficult in some parts of Africa, where the tradition of indigenous entrepreneurship is weak, but this should affect only the pace of change not the objective" (Accelerated Development p.65, 1981)

The Kenyan experience shows one way of tackling the issue of cyclical drought in parts of a country. "Food Aid" or importation of food is another, as advocated by the Wold Bank, which forwards the idea that African countries with a distinct comparative advantage in export crop production should import food if it is cheaper than it would cost to produce locally.

The problem of "food aid" is that it can undermine food security and destroy national food agriculture in that under SAPs farmers increasingly abandon traditional food crops at a time when there production is fundamental. For example in Zimbabwe during the Southern Africa drought of 1992 the country experienced a drop of 90% in it's maize crop, located largely in less productive lands. Yet at the height of the drought, tobacco for export (supported by modern irrigation, credit, research, etc) registered a bumper harvest. Furthermore much of the export earnings were used to service the external debt and not used to support subsistence agricultural infrastructure.

In order to manage cyclical drought governments have to formulate policies that promote self reliance through recognition of the policy demands of subsistence farming especially the role certain food crops play and the exchange relationship in the local economy. In Somalia for example any reforms to handle cyclical drought should have firstly considered the fragile exchange relationship between the "nomadic economy" and the "sedentary economy",—ie between pastoralists and small farmers characterised by money transactions as well as traditional barter. Failure to do so led do the destruction of the state and famine.

It is therefore clear to see that achieving policy outputs in agriculture is greatly influenced by externalities with the weather being the most influential. In order to achieve policy goals of feeding one's citizens policymakers have had to rely on external food aid with it's inherent risk of destabilising the domestic market.

In this regard it is important to note that total cereal food aid shipments under programme, project and emergency food aid in 1997/98 (July/June) are estimated to have reached at least 5.5 million tonnes worldwide. This represents an increase of some 3% from 1996/97, mainly on account of slightly larger shipments to low-income food-deficit countries (LIFDCs) resulting from more food emergencies, compared with the previous year, and additional food aid provision in response to the Asian financial crisis.

This increase in food aid flows is directly attributable to the deregulation of the grain market, which although in the short term leads to the prevention of famine, the policy output goals of raising agricultural production to the level of caput required to enhance the sector's contribution to economic development and food security is curtailed.

Indeed, FAO's per caput agricultural production index for sub-Saharan Africa (excluding South Africa) stood at 100 at the beginning of the 1990s (average for the period 1989–90), by 1996 it had not moved beyond 101.7, after which it fell back to 97.6 in 1997.

From it's economic projections, the IMF expects sub-Saharan Africa's policy outputs to improve, through improved macroeconomic policies and structural reforms, thereby bringing further gains in per caput GDP. However, among the major uncertainties in the IMF's economic growth projections for sub-Saharan Africa are the effects of the El Nino phenomenon on agricultural production as well as the possibility of declines in commodity prices (which may come about through food aid).

In assessing the policy outputs of a particular country, the IMF clearly gives the greatest emphasis and credit to the undertaking of economic reforms, which it believes leads to improved overall economic performance of which the agriculture sector is paramount. I have therefore picked on one East African country, Uganda which has undergone extensive reform to evaluate it's policy outputs.

Policy outputs: Uganda

Agriculture accounts for 44% of total output and 80% of employment, the agricultural sector is concentrated in the southern part of the country where the banana-coffee system and the Montane system of farming is practised.

(TABLE 5) shows the output of various agricultural products in Uganda.

—Export crops are coffee, coffon, tea and maize.

—Food crops are tubers and roots, maize, beans, sesame and sorghum. Almost half of agricultural production (19% of GDP) is traded or bartered for subsistence consumption outside the market system.

—It is important to note that subsistence production of agriculture still accounts for about 2/5 of agricultural output and 1/5 of total economic output.

TABLE 5. Agricultural Production in Uganda, 1996/97

Commodity	Volume ('000tonnes)	Percentage of total
Coffee	287925	88
Tea	16939	5
Plantains	9144	3
Tobacco	6349	2
Root crops	4111	1
Cereals	1588	0.5
Pulses	356	0.11
Nuts	285	0.09
TOTAL	326697	100

Source: Government of Uganda

Composition of Ugandan Exports

Uganda is Africa's leading coffee producer, in the early 1990s Uganda was in a good position to export due to substantial increases in international coffee prices. However high prices brought new producers into the market and production volumes have already increased bringing prices back down. Price weaknesses will continue to reduce export earnings from coffee.

Furthermore a new quality control system implemented by a major coffee trading company based in London may permanently harm the market for Ugandan coffee beans. Reports of excessive moisture in Uganda's coffee shipments may cause buyers to try other coffee producers now that new production is available. It is important to note that the prospects for the world coffee economy depend very closely on the evolution of the quantitative supply/demand ratios.

In this regard it is important to note that the prospects for consumption in the United States depends closely on the development of the so called "speciality coffee" which could help to reverse the decline in consumption by next year. In Europe, the development of new products such as exspresso coffee and gourmet coffees will ensure that consumption will remain high in many countries.

In order that Uganda's policy outputs regarding coffee meet the world demand, Uganda has taken a policy decision to develop high value gourmet coffee as opposed to only producing traditional high volume coffee. It has already developed liquor profiles for overseas buyers to select. This is likely to be a profitable undertaking both because customers are willing to pay a premium for coffee that exactly meets their needs and because high value business cannot be duplicated by high volume coffee producing competitors around the world.

Tea and cotton are the other important traditional export crops for Uganda. Compared to 1996 tea production rose in 1997/98. Cotton production on the other hand was adversely affected by drought in the early part of 1997, which curtailed planting and then the late season rains interfered with the transport of cotton to the ginning plants late in the year.

As agriculture is capable of generating strong backward and/or forward linkages, through processing and through other vertically integrated industries. Development of industry in Uganda through agriculture is a fundamental output of agricultural policy. The importance of forward linkages through agricultural processing is indicated in the Census for Business Establishments (manufacturing sector). The census covers establishments of 5 persons and above only. However most micro-enterprises in developing countries are in the size range of 1-4 persons (often 1-2).

The census shows (TABLE 6) that coffee processing, grain milling, tea processing, sugar and jaggery, and cotton ginning provided 37% of both value added and persons engaged.

Two further national resource-based activities, saw milling, wood and straw products and mineral products, nec (brick-making, etc), provided a further 4% of value added and 9% of persons engaged. The textile industry still has great potential if cotton growing can continue it's revival.

Table 6 Composition of Ugandan manufacturing in 1989

Activity	Employment		Value Added	
	No.	%	Sh.m.	%
Coffee processing	11097	20.6	7794	21.1
Textile goods	4378	8.1	2503	6.8
Furniture	3579	6.6	1393	3.8
Motor vehicle repair	3339	6.2	965	2.6
Sugar & jaggery	3266	6.1	3290	8.9
Grain milling	2870	5.3	1765	4.8
Non-metallic mineral prodn	2715	5.0	870	2.4
Spinning&weaving	2108	3.9	179	0.5
Beverages	2080	3.9	4103	11.1
Sawmilling	1970	3.9	657	>1.8
Tea processing	1744	3.2	367	<1.0
Fabricated metal products	1650	3.1	1529	4.1

Table 6 Composition of Ugandan manufacturing in 1989 (Continued)

Activity	Employment		Value Added	
	No.	%	Sh.m.	%
Chemical products	1255	2.3	2107	5.7
Cotton ginning	1137	2.1	582	<1.6
Tobacco products	719	1.3	3089	8.4
Total	53902	100	36994	100

Source: Census of Business Establishments, Manufactutring Sector (Establishments with 5 persons or more)

Demand Linkages Stemming From Agriculture

Demand linkages stemming from agriculture are important for the development of the rural small-scale enterprise. In this regard industrial development strategy must go hand in hand with agricultural development. The importance of the small scale sectors's potential for labour absorption has also been recognised by the Ugandan government. In the 1989 manpower survey report (MPED, 1989) it stated "The potential of the informal sector to continue to absorb large numbers of yearly additions to the labour force will depend largely on the extent to which the various constraints facing it are removed and official encouragement is given."

An interesting study (Twinomujuni, 1992) showed a wide range of linkages between the informal small scale engineering enterprises and equipment used in agro-based industries. These workshops based in Kampala and Jinja produced "capital goods" for agro-based industries (maize and rice mills, coffee hullers, oil presses, crop shellers, jaggery mills, crop threshers) and for agro-oriented industries (ploughs, feed mixers for poultry and dairy animal feed, grass choppers/cuffers).

It is important to note that while these products were not as professionally finished as their imported counterparts they were made at a fraction of the cost of the imported product thereby saving the country much needed foreign exchange.

As Uganda is a landlocked country with a substantial transport cost disadvantage coupled with a small market suggests that Uganda must pursue a strategy emphasising resource-based industrial development, maximising agriculture-industry linkages, small-scale industry, and "informal" urban and rural manufacturing geared to meeting the basic needs of the population.

POLICY OUTCOMES

The Politics of Food Crisis in Kenya

Policy outcomes or impacts are the consequences intended or unintended result-ing from political action or inaction. For instance the food crisises of 1979–80 and 1984–85 in Kenya led to the building of a new political regime in Kenya in a way that has not been seen on the continent before.

It is frequently assumed and argued that subsistence food crop crises are politi-cally destabilizing (e.g. Ethiopia, Somalia, and Zambia) but in Kenya the con-trary has happened. In the hands of a wily politician such as President Daniel Arap Moi, the subsistence crisis was used to destroy political enemies and forge political alliances.

During the Kenyatta presidency power was vested on the industrial base of multi-national corporations mostly located in Nairobi and in partnership with local entrepreneurs from Central Province (Kenyatta's power base). It was also based on export agriculture, in particular tea and coffee again mostly grown in Cen-tral Province and financed in part and protected by the national government.

Both those that worked in industry and those who drew their incomes from export agriculture consumed rather than produced the national staple maize. In promoting the economic fortunes of the Central Province the Kenyatta govern-ment transformed the relationship between the maize growing centre and the national government. The national government was now seen to be antagonistic to the domestic commercial agricultural producer especially the maize farmers.

In this regard the portion of the national bureaucracy whose mandate was to reg-ulate the grain industry the Maize Board was transformed from a defender of the interests of producers into a defender of low food prices. Following the death of Kenyatta in 1978 and the food crisis that followed the following year the new Moi regime had the opportunity to restructure the agricultural power base con-trolling the national government.

Moi and his followers come from the maize growing areas of the Rift Valley and Western Province and not from Central Province consequently their base lay not in the industrial and exporting regions. Consequently the threat of food shortages in the consuming regions (e.g. Central Province) provided the right opportunity for them to broaden their political base.

In the name of defending the interests of consumers the government was able to channel resource into the grain-growing areas and to consolidate powerful positions within them. This crisis enable the national government to revive and refinance the co-operative societies in the maize growing areas which became powerful political power brokers in these regions, it also enabled the government to multiply the resources available to political leaders in those areas.

The command and control tactics used by the Kenyan government to tackle the food crisis is interesting in that the policy outcome led to the consolidation of political power, whereas in other parts of Africa it has led to political disorder most notably in Somalia. In Kenya the policy demands for action to restructure the agricultural power base was inevitable when Kenyatta died. The food crisis offered the government "legitimate" power to take authoritative policy decisions to tackle the threat of hunger (which it did as a policy output) and in the process consolidated it's political power.

The Somalian Crisis

The origins and policy outcomes of the Somalian crisis are rooted in the economic reforms of the early 1980s that destroyed Somali agriculture. In the past Somalia was a pastoral economy based on "exchange" between nomadic herdsmen and small agriculturists. Nomadic pastoralists accounted for 50% of the population, livestock contributed 80% of export earnings until 1983, this was also boosted from the mid 1970s by cash remittances from Somali workers in the Gulf States bolstered by the oil boom. Food aid was non-existent in the early 1970s.

Through the IMF and World Bank a very tight austerity programme was imposed on the government largely to release the funds required to service Somalia's debt with the Paris Club. The SAP reinforced Somalia's dependency on imported grain as the donors were encouraging the development of so called "high value-added" fruits, vegetables, oilseeds and cotton for export, on the best irrigated farmland. Consequently from the mid-1970s to the mid 1980s, food aid increase 15 fold at the rate of 31% per annum. By the mid 1980s it was in excess of 35% of food consumption. (Farzin p265, 1991)

Like in the Kenyan case mentioned earlier the national government attempted a command and control measure to govern the country. Most notably in 1975 when a Land Reform Act was introduced which gave the ownership of all land to the state which would then regulate it's disposal and use. It could have been a progressive and constructive piece of legislation, but it turned on making registration of land the means of establishing the ownership of leaseholds. This procedure failed, on the one hand, to recognise the policy demands and complexities of customary Land Law and, on the other, the policy demands of those who did not work within contemporary western patterns of ownership.

Clauses within the legislation and the failure properly to control it, allowed the powerful, both legally and by fraud to register their ownership of huge amounts of land belonging, by customary law, to indigenous farmers. This land looting led directly to the various largely clan based, armed opposition groups, which were further supported by the new landless peasantry and by those farmers still in situ.

By the end of the 1980s land looting had displaced huge numbers of people and yet more fled in the face of a mobile and violent war, so they were dispossessed of, or driven away from precisely those resources which would have carried them through a time of drought. African Rights October 1993 makes a convincing case for the alienation of land as the principal cause of the famine of 1991–92. Furthermore international donors provided "aid" not in the form of capital and/or equipment but in the form of "food aid". This "food aid" would be sold by the government on the local market and the proceeds of these sales (i.e. "counterpart funds") would be used to cover the domestic costs of development projects. As of the early 1980s "the sale of food aid" and the counterpart funds generated from these commodity assistance programmes were the sole source of funding of development projects by the Somali government; most recurrent expenditure was also dependant on the donors.

The policy outcome of the simultaneous application of food "aid" and macro economic policy led to the destruction of food agriculture and nomadic pastoralism. Any importation of food for relief purposes should have been geared to the increasing purchase, at local market prices, of food produced within the country. Imported supplies should then have correspondingly been phased out. Since the early 1980s grain markets have been deregulated leading to a surplus on the international market, consequently the massive deliveries to Somalia amounted to an immense dumping operation which did massive damage to an indigenous agriculture.

Just how damaging this was is illustrated by the price of maize in one local market in the early months of 1993 when it fell to only 28% of the local cost of production (African Rights, May 1993). In the cases of rice, beans and oil, figures provided by ICRC Nairobi and CARE International Somalia, show market prices falling in August and September 1992 then fluctuating dramatically until May to June 1993 when the prices steadied at less than 6% of their high point in December 1992. (IOV 1994).

Unlike the Kenyan experience policy demands in Somalia were greatly influenced from outside it's national (political) system, mainly through the IMF and the World Bank. Policy decisions were dictated by international donors who ignored the country's agricultural social infrastructure.

Somalia could not undertake any meaningful agricultural policy as it was tangled in the straitjacket of debt servicing and structural adjustment. In 1989, debt servicing obligations represented 194.65 of export earnings. The macro-economic adjustment measures proposed by the IMF and the World Bank in the year prior to the collapse of the government of General Siyad Barre in January 1991 (at the height of the civil war) called for a further tightening over public spending, the restructuring of the central bank, the liberalisation of credit (which virtually thwarted the public sector) and the liquidation and divestiture of most of the state enterprises. In light of the above the collapse of the Barre government and any meaningful agricultural policy it may have had was now imminent.

In this era of globalisation the IMF and the World Bank's SAPs bear little direct positive influence on subsistence farming and may well support the process of famine formation because it systematically undermines all categories of economic activity whether urban or rural, which do not directly serve the interests of the global market system.

Throughout the continent agricultural policy decisions are increasingly coming under the control of the Bretton Woods institutions through "sectoral adjustment" which has unequivocally led to destruction of food security. Dependency vis-a-vis the world market has been reinforced, "Food Aid" to sub-Saharan Africa has increased by more than 7 times since 1974 and commercial grain imports more than doubled.

FAMINE

One cannot talk about the Somali crisis without looking into the issue of famines and food security. Famines in Africa have often triggered the "CNN Effect" most notable in Ethiopia in the 1980s and Somalia in the 1990s. Whereby the international community is bombarded by images of mass starvation. Such a perspective is problematic in that it tends to portray famine as a single event rather than as a process which culminates in significantly increased mortality rates.

Famine: "results from a sequence of processes and events that reduces food availability or food entitlements and causes widespread and substantially increased morbidity and morality" (Downing). Agricultural policy should therefore be geared to fostering food security. Over the last two decades the concept of food security has come to be the definitional scheme that considers the relationships between food production, distribution and consumption. The most widely used definition of food security is that outlined by the World Bank (1986):

Food security is access by all people at all times to enough food for an active, healthy life. Its essential elements are the availability of food and the ability to acquire it. Food insecurity, in turn, is the lack of access to enough food. There are two kinds of food insecurity: chronic and transitory.

Chronic food insecurity is a continuously inadequate diet caused by a household's persistent lack of ability to buy or produce enough food.

Transitory food insecurity is a temporary decline in a household's access to enough food. It often results from instability in food prices, declining food production or household incomes-and in its worst form produces famine.

The concept of food security can be further clarified by using the FAO definition where food security embraces three main objectives:

• Adequate supply (including production, reduction of post-harvest losses and balance between imports and exports)

• Stable supply (including production and price stability at interzonal and inter-temporal levels)

- Access to supply (including adequacy of consumption in the insecure zones, adequacy of income in relation to food prices and access to employment)

Using the FAO definition it is important to note that access to the supply of food is the key to understanding famines. In the past it was generally believed that the only cause of famine was a decline in food availability due to a reduction in production resulting from adverse weather, disease/pest infestation, or through a cutting-off of traditional sources of supply.

However, over the last century it is becoming evident that famines can occur in areas where overall food availability has not diminished, but as a result of a reduction in the ability of certain population groups to acquire food. This case was convincingly espoused by Amartya Sen in his book Poverty and Famines which outlined a conceptual framework for the analysis of people's ability to acquire food known as Entitlement Theory:

The term "entitlement" is used to signify command over resources which, in turn, give control over food or which can be exchanged for food. Through some combination of production, trade, labour, property rights, inheritance or social welfare provision, individuals have either direct access to food or the means by which to acquire it. Entitlements are not fixed or equal but vary according to an individual's position within a country or regional system of production, exchange, control and distribution.

The case of the Somali crisis has shown that despite huge infusions of international aid, the beneficiaries of this aid have not been able to exercise command over their resources. In other words the beneficiaries lost their entitlement, one cannot ignore the compelling correlation between massive international food aid and increasing vulnerability to famines.

Food aid arrives through a number of avenues. For instance all US food arrives under the authority of Public Law-480. This law provides three mechanisms for delivering food aid. Title II, which is emergency food is the most visible, as this is often shown on television in the western world. Title II food is also used regularly for food-for-work projects and nutrition programmes such as mother-child health and school feeding. These programmes are usually run by NGOs.

However a lot more food arrives in East Africa under Title III, which is "food for development". Under Title III commodities are sold in the recipient countries and the money used for development projects.

The largest part of PL-480 is Title I, wherby foods are sold to merchants at bargain-basement prices, at rates so low that they often don't even cover the cost of freight. Title I is administered by the US Department of Agriculture. Title I foods undermine farmers' attempts to get a fair price for their agricultural produce. Furthermore an additional factor often intrudes: Corruption.

Corruption: Almost all governments require that merchants are licensed to purchase foreign commodities. This has led to corruption, with permission to benefit from foreign and aid flows being bestowed as a factor upon loyal political allies and family members. In Somalia it was the president's inner circle who purchased all the grain.

It has been reported that every officer in the Somali Ministry of Agriculture were profiting from selling imported food at the detriment of the farmers, the very people they were supposed to help. And not only did food aid undercut farmers as mentioned earlier it also undercut legitimate Somali importers. An entire segment of the Somali busness community vanished as American and European cereals were sold at 50% to 60% less than they could have been purchased for.

Finally it is important to note that food security and agricultural policy in general are affected by debt. The debt burden on African countries remains a major constraint in developing viable food security programmes. For instance at the time of writing the World Bank had encouraged Malawi "to keep foreign exchange instead of storing grain".

Why, because one of Malawi's key commercial creditors had to have their debt repaid. In a BBC interview President Muluzi stated that his government "had been forced (to sell maize) in order to repay commercial loans taken out to buy surplus maize in previous years". The President went on to to say that the World Bank and IMF had "insisted that, since Malawi had a surplus and the (government's) National Food Reserve Agency had this huge loan they had to sell the maize to repay the commercial banks".

Consequently Malawi sold 28000 tonnes of maize the country's staple crop to Kenya for dollars. This is at a time when Malawi and other Southern African countries are in the thoes of a massive famine.

Malawi, like other African countries is having its economic programmes imposed on her by creditors, in Malawi's case this translates in the removal of farming and food subsidies therby putting food prices out of the reach of millions of poor people. It is not surprising that the Southern Africa Development Community (SADC) called for the cancellation of debts owed by six countries (Lesotho, Malawi, Mozambique, Swaziland, Zambia and Zimbabwe) where more than 14 million people are threatened by famine.

The debt situation weakens African economies especially countries experiencing famine such as those in southern Africa and in the Horn of Africa. This weakness allows creditors to use this opportunity to dispose of their surpluses and create food dependency. The following quotation by former US Secretary for Agriculture, Dan Glickman gives a good picture of a major donor, the USA and its attitude to countries suffering famine and in need of food aid:

"Humanitarian and national self interest both can be served by well-designed foreign assistance programmes. Food aid has not only met emergency food needs, but has also been a useful market development tool".

It is safe to say that so long as the budgets of African countries are targeted by creditors agricultural policy will be subject to their economic interests, programmes and priorities.

It is true that food aid may meet short term emergency food needs but it is seriously doubtful that food aid can contribute positively to sustainable markets and food security particularly in a climate where creditors exert a powerful influence on the budgets of African countries. For instance Ethiopia paid $100 million—nearly 10% of government revenues in 2002 to its creditors during its worst famine in 20 years. Zambia, Malawi and Mozambique are estimated to pay $250 million to their creditors in 2003, even as they struggle to feed their people.

This is inspite of a promise by G7 leaders in Cologne, Germany in 1999 to forgive the unpayable debts of the world's poorest countries, the relief was to be on top of the debts forgiven through the Heavily Indebted Poorest Countries HIPC process; under this debt relief deal 26 countries were supposed to have had $68bn of their debts written off by 2003. However, just over half that amount has been forgiven and the World Bank admits that for half of those countries the debt relief granted is not enough to make their debts sustainable.

IT is apparent that HIPC is floundering, the HIPC debt initiative first proposed in 1996 is an approach by the World Bank, IMF and governments around the world to reduce the external debt of the world's poorest, most heavily indebited countries. This initiative placed debt relief within the framework of poverty reduction.

The countries that qualify under HIPC such as Malawi, Ethiopia, Uganda and Zambia are eligible for highly concessional assistance from the International Development Association, IDA, the part of the World Bank that lends on highly concessional terms and from the IMF's Poverty Reduction and Growth Facility. Countries that also face an unsustainable debt situation even after the full application of debt relief mechanisms also qualify.

In 1999 a significant review of the original framework made it possible for countries that were not achieving debt sustainability through existing mechanisms to receive assistance under the HIPC Initiative. Under the new framework, sustainable debt-to-export levels are defined at a fixed ratio of 150% (on a net present value basis). But HIPC isn't working as planned, 10 of the 26 countries which entered HIPC since Cologne will exit with debt payments above that level.

Countries judged by the World Bank and IMF to have sustainable debts are still facing tremendous development. For instance when Ethiopia graduates from HIPC in 2003, payments to creditors will be reduced by about $30m but will still be half what it spends on its health system.

Another worrying trend is that debt is increasingly the result of private capital flows rather than "official" flows, and that private creditors tend to be resistance to restructuring when debt becomes "unsustainable". Many multinational firms involved in the agribusiness, agriculture and nutrition are likely to seek repayment regardless of the circumstances affecting the debtor country. A good example is the Swiss multinational Nestle which is claiming $73m in 2003 from the famine-stricken Ethiopian government.

According to the aid agency Oxfam $73m is enough to pay for food for 12 million people for a month. Furthermore Nestle was demanding $6m compensation from the Ethiopian, however it is important to note that the firm has pledged that the money it gets from its claims will go into famine relief efforts. This is a positive move that other creditors can emulate.

Although a lot more can and should be done to address the debt burden issue it is clear to see that of the 10 countries which have had payments reduced under HIPC are spending more on health and education. Health is a particular pertinent issue in regard to the food insecurity problem in Southern Africa. The HIV/

AIDS pandemic is making this famine particularly difficult to deal with given that a large percentage of the active population are too weak to plant, too weak to harvest; this is likely to be compounded by an anticipated El Nino year in 2003 which may lead to another drought.

But on a positive note President Bush's exhortation during his State of the Union address on the 28th of January, 2003, for Congress to commit $15 billion over five years to fight AIDS in Africa is a positive development. Although there is concern on the continent that the funding won't come quickly enough to address the emergency nature of the epidemic.

According to the White House, the President's request will not affect the 2003 budget and funds will only be available from 2004 with an increase of just $700 million. Of the $15 billion the President is proposing to spend over five years nearly $10 billion will be in "new money". If Congress approves that would roughly triple U.S. outlays over projected levels but this spending would not triple immediately. But in order to save lives this money must be made available immediately, large numbers for 2007 are meaningless to people who will die this year without access to essential anti-retroviral drugs.

The 2002–2003 U.S. budget for AIDS treatment and prevention programmes-domestic and foreign is a little more than $1 billion annually. What is required is at least $3.5 billion to be made available in 2003. Nevertheless as already stated this is the right step in the right direction which is likely to impact the the following African countries: Botswana, Cote d'Ivoire, Ethiopia, Kenya, Mozambique, Nambia, Nigeria, Rwanda, South Africa, Tanzania, Uganda and Zambia; which are the targeted countries under the President's Emergency Plan for AIDS Relief.

The President's initiative is intended to prevent 7 million new infections, provide anti-retoviral drugs for 2 million HIV-infected people and the care of 10 million HIV infected individuals and AIDS orphans. The AIDS initiative should be seen in light of Africa's development dilemma, sub-Saharan Africa spent $14.5 billion servicing foreign debts that is money that could have gone into basic education, health and particularly the fight against AIDS, malaria and tuberculosis. External debt is clearly making it very difficult for Africa to tackle economic and social development programmes. It is also important to note that the Presidents initiative must be accompanied with a commitment to ensure that African governments have access not only to affordable generic drugs but to compulsory licensing and parrellel imports agreements. So long as the U.S. continues to support the interests of the pharmaceutical companies in international trade negotiations Africans will not be able to afford these life saving drugs.

ETHIOPIA

Famine in the Horn of Africa has once again brought the question of whether food insecurity in Eastern Africa is a political, climatological or a technical problem. The answer is that famine is often a complex phenomenon and it encompasses various political, economic and geographical factors.

Ethiopia encompasses diverse agro-ecological zones, its rural population which is about 85% of the country's entire population is dependent on rain-fed agriculture for the livelihood. The direct cause of the Ethiopian food crisis is the failure of rain which in turn affects the ability of rural communities to withstand economic shocks such as drought. The Government of Ethiopia estimates that 10.2 million people will be in need of food aid in 2003.

Why is Ethiopia always in a food crisis? This is an important question particularly in an international climate that is more focused on other issues concerning international terrorism, the drought in Southern Africa and in light of donor fatigue. Nevertheless it is important to note that at the beginning of 2002 the food security situation in Ethiopia was better than average.

However, several conditions combined to contribute to the current food crisis. Firstly there was the failure of the short Belg (March to May) rains, although this was a set back the Ethiopian people were still hopeful that the long Meher (July to September) rains would be adequate and compensate for the Belg. The Meher rains were late and spotty which led to the current drought which affected areas such as West Hararghe Zone in Oromiya that has traditionall been considered the "breadbasket" of the zone and not usually threatened by drought.

Furthermore existing food relief programmes that were in place were based on the harvest of November/December 2001 and did not take into account the failure of the rains in 2002. Therefore the available food resources have been inadequate for the population in need.

To improve Ethiopia's food security situation both emergency preparedness and response capacity will continue to be the backbone of agricultural policy and development strategy. One of the most important aspects of a development strategy in drought prone areas is to increase the assets and entitlements of communities to enable them to withstand temporary disturbances in rainfall. To do this it is important to strengthen traditional collective organization, without ignoring social variables so as to build the social framework within which the envisaged policy can be implemented.

As mentioned earlier many donor countries have an excess of food, not cash and their food aid policies are designed in part to support their own agricultural production. In this regard famine-relief strategies are said to be food driven as opposed to need driven. Famine relief is required in Ethiopia but the country needs to follow a counter famine approach that incorporates the relevant social variables as a way of countering famine, combating malnutrition and address entitlement problems.

Counter-famine interventions are best implemented at the early stages of a crisis. Although Ethiopia is in the middle of a major drought counter famine interventionplans have to be in place that address financial assets (cash and savings); physical assets (livestock, tools, housing); human assets (skills, education, health) as well as strengthening community solidarity.

Without excluding relief aid counter-famine interventions are based on the premise that income and employment are the central issues that must be addressed in a a famine. Donors see food aid as an alternative source of food for starving Ethiopians, recipients view it in a wider context; they see it as income and a transfer of assets. That is why people will barter relief food for other commodities; for this reason food aid distributed to meet a nutritional targets rather than income security is likely to reduce the family's overall ability to recover both its income and food security.

The Ethiopian food problem is similar to that in other parts of sub-Saharan Africa in that food output per head is falling and this is one of the main factors contributing to hunger in Africa. As agriculture is the main source of livihood any decline in food output leads to the collapse of entitlements.

Given the chronic vulnerability of large parts of the Ethiopian countryside policy should be geared to improving assets as part of a long-term strategy, then protecting these asset in a time of crisis as a fundamental corollary element of development policy and strategy. In other words the current humanitarian relief programmes should not be "just relief", managed properly short term relief intervention can be incorporated in a long-term strategy to overcome poverty, reduce vulnerability and increase entitlement.

It is imperative that the long term strategy for Ethiopia distinguishes between;

1.   Food production as a source of income and entitlement and

2.   Food production as a source of supply or as a food commodity only.

In exploring ways of expanding food production (e.g through drought resistant crops) policy goals should primarily address the role of food production in generating entitlements rather than supply. Of course Ethiopia will need foreign assistance the question is will this foreign aid hinder or help the development of entitlements.

Ethiopia is one of the oldest nation states if not the oldest in Africa. It is a country that has endured political, economic and social turmoil that would have reduced any other country to the status of a failed state as is the case with Somalia. One of the greatest assets Ethiopia has is its human capital not only in country but also due to "brain drain" all around the world. If this human capital is matched with foreign resources a lot more can be achieved in addressing the current crisis.

Foreign resources alone will not lead to development as we have seen in Somalia which was almost entirely dependent on foreign assistance for development since its independence in July 1960. Somalia was one of the largest recipients of foreign aid during 1964–69 the annual average being approximately $15 per head of it's the 3 million people. This rate of aid is more than "three times then figure of $4.5 per capita", which according to the World Bank sponsored Pearson Commission Report (1970), represents the average annual aid to other developing countries during 1964–67.

In other developing countries foreign resources account for approximately 10% of total investment expenditure in Somalia 85% of Somalia's total development expenditure up to the end of 1969 was financed externally. This is an unusual case but it does offer countries like Ethiopia a unique opportunity to study the effectiveness of foreign assistance. Other African countries can ask what went wrong? What beneficial role did foreign aid make towards economic development? Were the wrong policies pursued by the Somali agreement that led to failure of foreign assistance.

Aid to Somalia was both project-tied and capacity tied. Under the project-tied aid Somalia was provided with a number of low-priority projects that did not contribute to the economic development of Somalia such as a university equipped to produce social science graduates only, rather than if it had been utilized in higher-priority projects such as land or livestock development.

Not only was aid to Somalia tied to specific projects it was also tied to the aquiring of goods and services from the donor countries only. Country tied aid diminishes the effectiveness of aid as an agent of development. According to United Nations studies conducted in a number of developing countries, tied aid makes the cost of goods and services some 15% to 25% more expensive and therefore is more beneficial to the donor.

George Woods, former president of the World Bank admitted, "to the extent that foreign aid is tied, it represents help for the exporters in the donor country.... Some countries have made it clear that they see development finance as nothing more than a disguised subsidy for their exporters" (The Guardian Manchester, 1 Aug 1967)

Although this book has concentrated on external factors affecting agricultural policy it goes without saying that the primary responsibility for development rests on the African countries themselves: aid is best used as a supplement to the full mobilization of domestic resources including human capital. In the case of Somalia the ambitious First Five Year Plan 1963–1967, which was estimated at a total of $200 million gave relatively low priorities to engines of development such as health, water supplies, transport and education.

Furthermore the Somali government misused the foreign aid proceeds through corruption, maladministration and the undertaking of economically unviable projects. For example, the Short Term Two Year Development Programme launched in 1968 to consolidate the work of the first plan admits to this fact and was highlighted in the Economist, 25 Febuary, 1984.

This state of affairs is not unusual in Africa and has already been alluded to earlier in the context of the post-colonial state and the cold war. In addressing the food insecurity problems in Ethiopia one cannot help but to notice that the relationship that has been established between foreign capital, major id giving bodies and local power elite has not been dissimilar to the situation in Somalia. Both countries have had the experience of being patronized by the Soviet Union and the

United States during the cold war, which not only led to superpower inspired proxy wars but to relationships that often led to projects which have not been in the best interest of economic and social development.

Nevertheless Ethiopia has the potential and capacity to overcome its current difficulties. The problem in Ethiopia as in other parts of Africa is that most of the crisis is related to erratic weather patterns. According to the World Disaters Report: 2002, "the past two years have seen the highest number of weather-related disasters reported over the decade". This is further compounded by the AIDS pandemic, civil strife and issues related to governance and economic policies.

Countries like the United States blame the famine squarely on the government and contend that in averting this and future disasters adequate levels of assistance must be provided immediately and in the medium to long term technological inputs and innovations is the key to boosting agricultural productivity (United Nations Security Council, 4652nd Meeting). Biotechnology has been a controversial issue in Southern Africa and has received less attention in Ethiopia and in the Horn of Africa nevertheless it is a issue that needs addressing.

BIOTECHNOLOGY

A lot has been made of the potential of biotechnology alleviating food insecurity in Africa, while certainly important biotechnology is unlikely to generate another Green Revolution in the six major food staples crops (maize, cassava, sorghum, millet, wheat and rice) as was the case in Asia during the 1960s. The Green Revolution in Asia was based on input-responsive semi-dwarf varieties sometimes called Modern Varieties or MVs. When these MVs were grown with increased levels of fertilizers and a reliable water supply yields increased providing higher incomes (entitlements) to farmers allowing the vast population of the Asian sub continent to be fed from a comparatively small area under cultivation.

Could Asia's Green Revolution model address Africa's food crisis? The answer is sadly no, firstly because the Asian model was based on only two food crops grown under irrigation while 90 to 95% of food production in Africa is rainfed. Secondly, unlike Asia where two dominat food crops are grown in large homogenous areas under irrigation, Africa has a multitude of food crops grown under diverse ecologies with serve and erratic weather. The nature of the crop creates its own policy demands as mentioned in the beginning of this book.

Policy issues in regard to biotechnology has been mainly in regard to the whole-kernal biotechonolgy maize. African countries, particularly Zimbabwe are concerned that these Genetically Manufactured Organisms (GMOs) may have negative effects on human health and/or the enviroment. In addition African countries are wary of the agribusiness private sector in the West and consequently question proprietary tools and products produced by these agribusiness multinationals. Furthermore considering the vast sums invested in biotechnology research most of the multinational involved in biotechnology are unlikely to grant access to their proprietary tools and products and if they do they require licensing fees, royalty payments and material transfer. This in turn leads to the issue of tied aid.

Policy makers have therefore had to look for African solutions to Africa's food crisis; one of the countries policymakers have looked at is Zimbabwe despite its current malaise. In the past Zimbabwe has shown innovative technological initiatives that generated two maize revolutions: the first was led by large-scale commercial farmers in the 1960s and 1970s. The second was launched by smallholders after independence in 1980.

Technological breakthroughs in agriculture have long gestation periods but offer a long run solution to food insecurity. For example in the U.S. research expenditures on hybrid corn began in 1910, but it was not until the 1930s did corn production become widespread. Developing new technology by "borrowing" scientific knowledge from abroad and blending it with indigenous technology also takes some time but can lead to innovative breakthroughs, given that a high level of scientific knowledge and aptitude are present. As mentioned earlier in regard to Ethiopia the role of Africa's human capital abroad can contribute to innovative breakthroughs in agriculture as was the case in Zimbabwe.

Zimbabwean scientists have led the way in developing an innovative way of using foreign technology in order to bring about a food crop revolution. The scientists found the inbred and hybrid maize lines from the Corn Belt of the United States were not suited to the agroecology of Zimbabwe. They therefore imported varities from Central America and South Africa and crossed them with local varieties. This approach after 28 years of research did not only lead to the acclaimed SR52 in 1960, a high-yielding maize variety that increased maize yields on farms by 46% (without fertilizer) over the yield of Southern Cross, the most common improved local open pollinated variety; but to the development in the 1970s of

R200, R201 and R215 hybrids for low-rainfall areas where a high proportion of smallholders live.

The SR52 hybrid maize is without doubt the most famous improved food crop variety that has ever been developed in Africa. It was quickly adopted by Zimbabwean commercial farmers on fertile land with high rainfall consequently maize production grew rapidly in the 1960s and 1970s. The government also enhanced its capacity to manage a national maize economy in times of scarcity and abundance through an integrated maize production and marketing system.

Zimbabwe's integrated maize extension and distribution system turned maize into a cash crop that enabled the country to export maize for 19 to 21 years over the 1970–91 period. This was an important development because traditionally biotechnology initiatives in addressing food supply problems have often been in the domain of individual countries; that is individual countries were responsible for their own food security only. Each country was responsible for their own food production, trade rarely enters into the scenario. The case of Zimbabwe proves that specialization, biotechnology and trade initiatives can contribute to solving food insecurity across national boundaries.

However it is important to note that increases in maize production does not automatically translate to access to food entitlement. Entitlement or food access issues are of critical importance as mentioned earlier and have to be incorporated and addressed at the policy level when formulating a comprehensive agricultural policy.

Zimbabwe's second maize revolution doubled the smallholders maize production in 6 years (1980–86) by using hybrid maize varieties and fertilizer. This revolution attracted considerable international attention not only because it was led by smallholders but it occurred during the Ethiopian famine (1984–85). The doubling of maize production is attributed to several factors including peace in the countryside after a bitter war, the removal of racial and institutional barriers to credit and expansion of subsidized government marketing services.

Zimbabwe has gone through difficult food policy scenarios ranging from a food surplus in the mid-eighties to a drought in 1992, food riots in Harare in 1998 and famine in 2002. How could a country that showed such promise sink to the depths it finds itself in at the beginning of a new century?

The answer lies in the subset of political and macroeconomic factors. Firstly the economy began faltering in the late 1980s and early 1990s under the weight of mis-managed money-losing state industries and heavy food subsidies. Under pressure from international financial institutions the government pursued economic policy reforms with the goal of liberalizing and privatizing the food system and opening up the market economy; given the state of the Zimbabwean economy these reforms did not translate into greater entitlements to rural Zimbabweans.

Secondly, the expropriation of about half of the country's private land, most of it owned by whites by President Mugabe as a way to reverse the pattern of land ownership has only excercebated the food security problem, during a severe drought.

What can African countries learn from the Zimbabwean experience? Firstly policy makers and donors should turn inward and examine Africa's own production success stories starting with those of hybrid maize in Zimbabwe, Kenya and Zambia. In the past it has been customary to draw lessons from Asia's Green Revolution without much success due to fundamental differences between Africa and Asia in terms of their agroecologies, crop diversities and stages of scientific and institutional development.

It is important to note that in the late 1950s and early 1960s Africa was a net exporter of food while Asia was experiencing a food crisis. It is for this reason that policy makers in Africa during a climate of favourable food security gave priority to industrial development while ignoring the agricultural sector.

Africa's food balance sheet changed in the early 1970s. From 1970 to 1985 annual food production grew at half (1.5%) of population growth (3.0%). Famine in the Sahlian region in West Africa and other short-term food emergencies led to Africa becoming a net importer of food. This combination of short term food emergencies and stagnation in long-term food production was very similar to the chronic food crisis that had affected India and other Asian countries in the 1960s and 1970s.

In conclusion African countries need to develop an indigenous capacity to deal simultaneously with short-term food emergencies and long-term growth in food production. Food production in many countries will have to come from raising crop yields rather than through area expansion in order to feed an increasing population. It is also important to note that food security cannot be achieved through a single input; rather like in Zimbabwe a comprehensive integrated system of institutions have to be formulated and coordinated to boost agriculture production and link the agriculture to other development goals such as trade while addressing the issue of entitlements. In the past African countries have concentrated on one or two magic bullets (e.g credit) and assumed that food security can be achieved in a few years.

POLICY IMPLICATIONS AND IMPACT: AGRICULTURAL MARKET REFORM

What can Africa do to reform the agricultural sector so as to eliminate the existing biases against the sector. During the 1980s when many countries in sub-Saharan Africa were in the thoes of structural adjustment and stabilization programmes, agricultural market reforms received considerable emphasis. The Berg report provided the framework for these market reforms.

This chapter tries to assess the impact of the reforms on the agricultural sector and the overall performance of African countries in East Africa. Given the large amount of case studies conducted in sub-Saharan Africa on major agricultural markets, I have not attempted to include all the findings but a rather to illustrate the main findings so as to draw out the policy implications.

Agricultural market reforms comprise of the following:

- Removal of regulatory controls on input and output markets (allowing the private sector in the agricultural marketing of inputs and products)

- Liberalization of input and output prices by eliminating or reducing subsidies on agricultural inputs such as fertilizers and credit

- Restructuring of public enterprises and the withdrawal of marketing boards from pricing and marketing activities.

Firstly it is important to note that agricultural market reforms were at the forefront of the the majority of the post 1984 structural adjustment programmes in sub-Saharan Africa. The market reform measures were based on the premise that since the agricultural has a large and higher share of tradables compared with other economic sectors (excluding the mineral and energy sector), an improved terms of trade brought about by liberalization would lead to a boost in agricultural supply. This entailed the abolishing of state control over agricultural marketing.

However, market reforms varies across African countries and in many cases reforms were only partially implemented and policy reversal was common. For example fertilizer subsidies in many countries were eliminated only in mid-1990s, and in several crop sectors parastals remain active e.g maize markets in Malawi, Zimbabwe and Kenya. Incomplete reform implementation makes it difficult to assess policy impact especially in light of civil unrest and conflict in countries such as Rwanda and the Democratic Republic of Congo, the prevalence of HIV/AIDS further complicates the task. Nevertheless at the risk of generalization it is still possible to assess the impact of reform policies on agricultural input and output markets namely the fertilizer, food crop and export crop markets.

Fertilizer

Reforms affecting the fertilizer sector vary widely. In regard to subsidies, Kenya and Zimbabwe never had prominent fertilizer subsidies, although they had price controls and import restrictions until the 1990s, whereas in Tanzania and Malawi subsidies continued into the 1990s. Malawi is an interesting case in that the government attempted to reduce and eventually eliminate subsidies over 1985–88, but abandoned the policy in the second year owing to poor rains and a large devaluation. Fertilizer subsidies were then removed in 1995–96, but the new Starter Pack Initiative is in place and it involves free distribution of small amounts of fertilizer and seed to smallholders.

Although parastatals have been marginalised in the distribution of fertilizer in Kenya, Tanzania and Uganda; they are active in Malawi and Zimbabwe. In Malawi, the Agricultural Development and Marketing Corporation (ADMARC) is a prominent distributor of fertilizer to smallholder farmers; and in Zimbabwe two state enterprises produce fertilizer and a third dominates fertilizer distribution however it is important to point out that these parastatals compete with private firms as is the case in Zambia where private firms compete with the national Food Reserve Agency.

In Ethiopia, fertilizer subsidies have been phased out and distribution liberalized, although regional governments play a significant role in that a number of "private" firms companies with close affiliations with regional authorities tend to dominate distribution; furthermore the National Extension Programme (NEP) provides inputs on credit at low interest rates to millions of small farmers, making NEP the largest buyer and distributor of fertilizer in the country.

In summary it is safe to say that most African countries have eliminated universal subsidies, liberalized fertilizer importation to private firms as part of there structural adjustment and stabilization programmes. Nonetheless, the state continues to be involved in fertilizer markets in many countries.

It is also apparent that the results of fertilizer market reform have been less positive than expected by the proponents of structural adjustment and liberalization however the impact has been less negative than is generally perceived. The reforms have fallen short in the following respects:

- The cost savings associated with privatized markets were not sufficient to prevent fertilizer prices from rising in response to subsidy removal and devaluation

- Growth in fertilizer use has been slow in the post-reform period, and fertilizer use has fallen in some countries

On the otherhand, fertilizer market reform has fufilled the expectations of proponents in that:

- Private firms have emerged to fulfill the functions formerly carried out by parastatals and government ministries at significant cost savings contrary to the fears of those who argued that the private sector was not sufficiently developed.

- The elimination of the fiscal burden associated with fertilizer subsidies has contributed to smaller fiscal deficits and, indirectly to macroeconomic stabilization in many countries.

Food Market Reform

Since the early 1980s, donors and multilateral agencies have advocated food market reforms as a central component of overall structural adjustment programmes. Over the past two decades reforms enacted by African countries have gone beyond the relatively limited reform agenda set forth by the World Bank's Berg

Report; and significant achievements in food market reform include the increased entry by private traders into food trade, reduced marketing margins and increased producer prices.

However, food plays a dual purpose, serving both as a source of producer income and as an urban and rural wage good, this conflict between the two purposes highlights the food policy dilemma that confronts food market liberalization. Governments, particularly in Eastern and Southern Africa are constantly battling with the need to support the rural smallholder and increase producer prices and with the need to provide cheap food for urban populations.

Nonetheless the main aim of structural adjustment and food market reform in particular has been to improve the performance of the smallholder sector. Consequently reform efforts have been geared to expanding marketed surpus, primarily through the effect of increased producer prices. However, although the initial aim of food market reform was to provide price incentives to rural producers, pressures emerged later on to keep consumer prices low. The contradictory effects of the two objectives led to a third objective: decreasing the costs of marketing.

Market reform is largely predicated on the premise among donors that marketing boards in Africa depressed food production by taxing agriculture. This is generally true in the case of coarse grains in Central Africa and in the non maize-based regions of Eastern Africa. Food policy on the otherhand in maize-dependant countries of Eastern and Southern Africa, where state intervention was significant and based on extensive subsidization of European settler producers as well as of African smallholders was fundamentally different.

In these countries, urban food security depended to a greater extent on domestically produced white maize, rather than on imported grain such as rice and wheat as is the case in Central Africa. In maize dependent states of Eastern and southern Africa the government played an important role in providing credit and input and output markets, it therefore becomes difficult to assess the impact of market reforms vis a vis production. But it is still important to ask how successful has market reform in Sub-Saharan Africa been? Given the objectives of removing distortions in the agricultural economy caused by rent seeking and biases and the reduction or elimination of unsustainable fiscal costs of state intervention.

The main impact of reforms include a reduction in the fiscal costs of the marketing system, to the extent that official prices are aligned with the market. However they has been a limited impact on grain production and agricultural productivity, the reforms have also increased price instability for both producers and consumers.

Although market reform have had a positive impact on market performance by reducing marketing and processing costs, and improving the spatial integration of markets. Agricultural markets still face high transport costs, low levels of investment and specialization by private traders and the market lacks the sophisticated arrangements and practice of a well developed commodity market that includes among other things forward selling procedures.

Generally speaking the reform policy has taken a negative view of the role of the State, a consensus is emerging that is of the opinion that the State can, and should, play a positive role in enhancing market development beyond reform. Thus, some donors' approach, for example in Tanzania and Zambia, has been to support state-dominated cooperation. It is clear that as market reform moves to market development the State's role in forming an institutional infrastructure or regulatory framework that encompasses legal and social conventions about transactions and contracts between individuals is crucial.

Market Reforms for Export Crops

Reform of export crop markets was motivated by the inability of governments to maintain parastatals and producer prices at a time of falling world prices following the oil shock of 1973. This price decline did not affect tropical beverage crops because of a tripling of their prices in 1976–77 marketing season. By 1979, however, commodity prices were widely in decline. It is these commodity price swings that contributed to the inauguration of structural adjustment programme lending by the World Bank in 1979.

Africa's main agricultural exports are accounted for by ten commodities: cocoa, coffee, cotton, tobacco, sugar, tea, palm oil, rubber, bananas and peanuts, these products account for more than 90 % of the continents exports. The remaining 10 % is split among a number of non traditional exports, these cover specialty products important for some countries (such as cashews in Tanzania and cut flowers in Kenya).

The heavy concentration of Africa's traditional exports in and within agriculture has been a perennial concern of African policymakers. Indeed opposition to the

Berg report's proposition for structural adjustment is influenced by the view that SAPs are a strategy of further concentrating resources in agricultural exports an over invested sector at the expense of other areas of the economy.

The evidence is that SAPs as a whole has probably favoured the diversification of economies somewhat out of agriculture. Countries that diversified their agricultural exports were successful at expanding production in the first half of the 1990s. In Uganda, for example, non traditional agricultural exports increased from US$ 1.4 million in 1988 to US$ 75 million in 1993 (World Bank, 1996).

However, almost US$ 20 million of this was in maize and bean exports to Kenya (which was experiencing a drought) that was unsustainable once the rains in Kenya returned. Another big component fish exports to Europe has not been sustained because of health bans imposed by the European Union

In general it is safe to say that non traditional exports continue to offer promise, but numerically are not likely to be enough to offer an alternative to traditional agricultural exports for some time. It is ironic to note that export market liberalization promotes diversification of total exports, reducing over-reliance on agriculture commodity exports and it clearly promotes overall growth at the expense of agriculture.

Ideally the overall growth will diversify domestic food demand, but in the case of some countries particularly Rwanda and Uganda exports of non traditional commodities "acquired" in the Democratic Republic of Congo have not stimulated the domestic food economy and has not benefited Ugandan society as a whole.

The prospects of export crop reform in the future are uncertain. Although the prospects for worldwide recovery are good (World Bank, 2000), price falls for Africa's main exports of the order of 50-60 percent since 1997 due to the nearly simultaneous disasters for world commodity markets arising from the Asian economic crisis starting in July 1997 and the Russian financial crisis starting in August 1998 will take some time to resolve.

The implementation of market reforms and their impact on agricultural growth have varied across countries, and results have been less than expected but some progress has been achieved in most cases. As mentioned earlier market reforms of the 1980s were geared on reducing government intervention in agricultural markets and increasing the producer price of tradable agricultural commodities. Aid donors and policymakers at the time were under the impression that improving farmers' price incentive and liberalizing markets would be enough to generate a supply response and efficient markets.

It is now evident that price reform alone is not enough to boost Africa's economies. What is needed is longer term investment initiatives that deal with privatization, institution building and infrastructure development. These are complex tasks and are not easy to implement given the short term nature of policymaking.

The actual implementation of market reforms have rarely been fully implemented. Many governments have liberalized internal domestic trade but have continued to dominate external trade. In Southern and Eastern Africa governments have continued to control food crop marketing, this is in light of the overriding concern over food security and the thin world market for white maize. Marketing boards are also still active in Malawi, Kenya and Zimbabwe.

It is also important to note that for the most part reforms were implemented in a top-down fashion without the participation of key groups such as private entrepreneurs, NGOs and civil servants. This created uncertainity about the motives of governments thereby rendering implementation less sustainable.

One of the purposes mentioned earlier of market reform is to improve the incentive structure of smallholder farmers through higher prices so as to lead to a positive supply response, thereby raising aggregate agricultural output and overall income. In this regard reforms have had a beneficial impact in there has indeed been a positive supply response; more evident however in export crops than for food crops mainly because liberalization has moved relative prices in favour of tradables and the use of imported inputs such as fertilizer has become more profitable for export crops such as coffee in Uganda.

It is however, still too early to evaluate the total impact of market reforms on agricultural supply given the fact that most Sub-Saharan African countries did not implement reform until the early to mid 1990s. Nevertheless the net gainers so far from reforms have generally been producers with a marketable surplus and consumers and producers close to urban markets.

CONCLUSIONS

Agricultural policy demands in Africa today could be viewed as a debate on strategy that advocates food self-sufficiency on one hand and export promotion on the other. Critics of export production fear that the production of agricultural exports will increasingly be controlled by an expanded agribusiness, and thus lead to an increase in rural poverty and hunger through competition between food and export crops for for scarce capital, land and other inputs, and through a growing consolidation of land ownership and control which decrease the access of small farmers to the land and create a larger rural proletariat.

Agricultural policy in Africa has in the past suffered from the urban-industrial biases of the 1940s and 1950s, development planners tended to think of agriculture as a "bargain basement" (a phrase associated with India's PM Nehru in the 1950s) and consequently agricultural policy largely proposed urban solutions to essentially rural problems.

This philosophy has had a great impact on agricultural policy and the Lewis 2 sector model seems to emasculate this philosophy perfectly. In his classic work on economic development with unlimited supplies of labour (Lewis 1954), Lewis wrote of massive disguised unemployment in the traditional, rural sectors of LDCs and urged rural to urban migration as a costless way of transferring labour to more profitable enterprises in the "modern" sector.

However since Lewis' 2 sector model the prevailing orthodoxies have often been challenged. This dissertation has attempted to highlight some of these challenges, such as the development of Rural Non-Farm income and the role of farmer education in boosting rural development.

The influence of the prevailing models and orthodoxies on agriculture development in Africa come about through the direct influence of the Bretton Woods institutions namely the World Bank and the IMF. This study has tried to show that through these institutions the incorporation of the poorer countries into the global economic system has radically transformed land use practices and has also firmly established unsustainable development practices.

The 1980s and 1990s has again seen challenges to the prevailing view of agricultural policy and development in general by Africans themselves. In 1987 African scholars from many disciplines met together in Kericho, Kenya under the auspices of Nairobi based African Academy of Sciences and the Dakar-based Council for Development of Economic and Social Research in Africa (CODESRIA). They established the Beyond Hunger Project as a counter to what they called the "self-fulfilling" prophecies of an Africa in permanent crisis.

They challenged all the conventional wisdom on Africa, of state centred, directive, donor driven, capital intensive projects and proclaimed a vision of grass roots orientated, locally initiated, people intensive programmes. In their view agricultural policy should be linked with the liberation of women, intellectuals and ethnic minorities from neglect and oppression and in new adaptations of technological innovations to African conditions and finally in broader regional associations and new forms of pan-African unity.

This initiative was followed within 2 years by the UN Economic Commission for Africa (UNECA) report "African Alternative to Structural Adjustment Programmes: A framework for Transformation and Recovery". This report was the direct response to the world bank report "Africa's Adjustment and Growth in the 1980s". The UNECA report emphasised that human beings and not institutions or markets must be the "fulcrum for development" which must involve "the extended family for the co-operative spirit of self-help development and traditional sanctions on leadership".

The UNECA programme has been criticised for it's lack of practicality and it's continued reliance on government intervention in place of the market. (Pickett and Singer, 1990). But government intervention is not necessarily a bad thing as was the case in Kenya during the 1979–80 and 1984–85 food insecurity crisises.

The search for African solutions by Africans in face of the influence of the World Bank and the IMF is not a new idea. In 1980, the Lagos Plan of Action for Africa's development towards economic unification by the year 2000 had been prepared for the OAU. It was a response to the failure of African governments to obtain protection against the declining world prices of their exports through help from a common fund for commodities, which was established by the UN conference on Trade and Development (UNCTAD). The Lagos Plan was countered by a World Bank report "Accelerated Development in Sub-Saharan Africa: An

Agenda for Action" proposing to supply funds to individual governments which adopted SAPs.

It is clear to see that the African initiatives are geared to tackling food insecurity and seeking protection against the declining world prices of their exports. Agricultural policy seems to be affected by two opposing doctrines; one from outside the continent and another from within. In this regard it is also important to note it is not only the World Bank and the IMF which have advocated the export of primary commodities. A study by the UN Secretary General's Expert Group on Africa's commodity problems provided similar advice:

"During the course of economic development, the relative importance of the commodities sector invariably declines over time. The speed with which it declines is a product of development itself. In the African context, the most obvious route to overall transformation is thus, paradoxically, to strengthen the commodities sector...the required changes will not take place without a macro economic policy and institutional framework that enable and encourages product expansion, productivity growth and increased competitiveness" (UN, 1990)

However, this "macroeconomic policy and institutional framework" that will foster agricultural productivity growth is seen by many African experts as probably the most damaging aspect affecting Africa's rural development. Somalia's experience shows that the application of macro economic policies and setting up of an institutional framework that ignores the policy demands of nomadic pastoralism can lead to the collapse of civil society.

These macro economic policies affecting agriculture are based on the farmer's responsiveness to price alone without much thought being given to other variables. For instance in Kenya, most farmers prefer growing horticultural products because of the low cost and high returns of the crop at the expense of traditional exports and food crops. This focus on price incentives alone may carry environmental risks. For example, intensive carnation production in Kenya represents the introduction into the tropics of a temperate plant which, due to its lack of natural immunity, normally necessitates the heavy use of agro-chemicals. Their residues drain into Lake Naivasha. If concentrations of agricultural pollutants build up they could harm the rich fauna of that Lake, one of Kenya's tourist attractions. If ecological damage were to proceed unchecked the economic costs of luxury export crops of exotic origin, measured in foreign-exchange earnings, could outweigh the benefits.

Furthermore the prevailing view of Africa's scholars is that the gap created by liberalisation policies reducing state involvement in the economy is being filled by plundering privateers and that the co-operative principle must establish itself in both rural and urban economies not necessarily as an alternative to the private entrepreneur, but as the leading force in the empowerment of the agricultural producers upon which Africa's development depends (Adedeji, 1973). This translates at the local level in the strengthening of African NGOs and rural institutions to hold together smaller associations on a democratic basis, sometimes working in partnership with foreign NGOs.

Given the current food crisis it is unmistakably clear that Africa's agricultural sector is not developing. Food shortfalls have necessitated the importation of grain and these in turn increased the financial burden on countries. Conventional wisdom states that there is little reason to believe that the need for food imports will end soon and in this regard there is a tendency to treat food aid less and less as humanitarian assistance whereby costs are borne by the donor and more and more as a straight market transaction whereby costs will be borne by the recipient country.

Africa's agrarian stagnation extends to the export sector. The crisis of development is directly linked to the poor performance in the export sector. To participate in the global economy African countries export primary agricultural products and import finished goods. Classical economic theory supposes that the relative value of commodities is determined by the amount of labour involved in their production, consequently it is clear to see that exporting primary products particularly agricultural products puts Africa at a disadvantage in the interanational market.

Most of African exports are intrinsically of less value than imported manufactured goods for the simply reason that less human labour is involved in their production. Therefore if the basic presupposition of this labour theory of value is valid then current trade systems can only damage African development in that African countries can never create or return an economic surplus large enough to finance the growth of the agricultural sector or the capitalization of an industrial programme.

Furthermore an important point to note is that agricultural exports have traditionally benefited western businesses particularly the multinational processing and merchandizing firms that deal in commodities such as coffee, tea, cocoa and cotton. It is in the interest of these multinationals to push primary agricultural prices downwards so as to increase profits. These firms posses a powerful influence in the international trade system and are often able to acquire the products they need on their terms

The above not withstanding agricultural surplus has also been used to fund the life style patterns of Africa's bourgeois classes. Military spending by governments have diverted much needed local and hard currencies further weakening fragile economies. The policies of African governments may indeed be responsible for a weak agricultural base and consequently these governments may be held more accountable than western governments and multinationals.

Nevertheless Africa's agraian crisis is founded on the concept of unequal exchange, in other words declining terms of trade. A low demand elasticity for primary agricultural exports in the international economic environment combined with protectionist policies by western governments which impose tariffs and duties that rise with the degree of value-added manufacturing makes an export-led growth strategy advocated in the Berg Report highly unlikely.

Low demand elasticity of primary agricultural exports means that even drastic price cuts in such commodities such as coffee is not likely to increase demand in the importing countries. Therefore lower prices with no increase in export volumes only impact agricultural output negatively by increasing the cost of imported inputs such as pesticides and chemical fertilizers.

In analyzing agricultural policy the role of African governments is central to understanding the systematic bias against the agricultural sector. Governments are greatly influenced by the urban elites because urban inflation and unemployment as opposed to rural poverty is a great destabilizer of African regimes; it is not surprising therefore that in order to survive governments have treated agriculture as an inexhaustible resource to cater to the needs of the urban sector.

However, given the malaise of the agricultural sector and liberalization polices that have reduced State involvement in the economy; plundering privateers have moved in to fill the gap. But these privateers are not interested in the stagnant agricultural economy but in Africa's higher value primary products: minerals

In today's neo-liberalism world where the main thrust of monopolistic finance capital is in continuous search for markets and profits, agriculture is being relegated in favour of more rewarding endeavours, In order to cater to the urban elite some African countries have formed alliances with foreign capital, mainly mining and energy companies which protect their investments with Private Military Companies (PMCs). Some analysts contend that this trend is likely to increase in the post-cold war arena especially in countries where agriculture is unable to support its citizens.

The Rwandan and Ugandan armies in eastern Congo have often been justified by Kigali and Kampala on the grounds of national security; however the economic stakes are just as important as the security issues. In an interview with the New Yorker an adviser to Rwandan President Paul Kagame stated "America can live without the Congo. Rwanda cannot…By itself, ours is a non-viable country". This summarises the situation of a country based on agricultural exports.

Rwanda the most densely populated country in Africa had an annual growth rate of 3.1% a year in the period 1980–1990 this had an adverse effect on an already unstable and fragile political and economic environment. At first agricultural production kept pace with population growth but by the mid to late 1980s poor growing conditions and decreasing fertility of the soil reduced returns to farmers.

An increase in the numbers of landless cultivators and the fall in agricultural productivity in a country where 90% of the population lived from farming created an unsustainable economy of which agriculture offered nothing that would lead to growth and development. The early 1980s also saw the start of a new boom in mineral and energy exploration on the continent; given the returns in trading in minerals and energy; predominantly agricultural exporting countries like Rwanda and Uganda have involved themselves in the mineral extraction business.

Kigali's elite living beyond the means of the country have now made the riches in the Congo essential to maintaining their livihood. Rwanda exports diamonds though it produces none, it exports coltan far in excess of its national production, it also has a office for "production" which deals with commercialization and trade issues including looted resources from the Congo. The office of production is firmly entrenched in the External Security Organization, ESO a powerful forum that influences government policy and highly biased against agriculture.

Uganda, the West's darling and the first country to graduate from HIPC has fallen back into unsustainable debt at a time of collapsing coffee prices, Uganda's predominant export. Uganda now controls the gold mines of Kilo-Moto in the Congo among other mines and is using this looted wealth to finance the life-style patterns of middle and upper class elite groups which are enjoying a level of personal consumption that is disproportionate to the economic capacity of the Uganda society. The state of affairs in Uganda and Rwanda have led to the term "warehouse-state" a term first coined by B. Hibou that appropriately defines a State that profits handsomely from serving as a transit point for legal and illegal exports from neighbouring countries.

Although the complexity of the Congo crisis are beyond the scope of this book, it is important to address conflicts in Africa if one is to create a suitable environment so as to achieve peace whereby sustainable development policies can be implemented. It is also imperative to underscore some of the motivations driving predominately agricultural countries into mineral extraction operations and the inevitable international consequences. African countries often cite security issues as pretext to invade neighbouring countries but economic considerations appear paramount.

The vast profits available in mineral extraction have led to the convergence of interests between the Uganda regime and the donor community. This explains Uganda's privileged position, despite the criminal activities of the Ugandan State in the Congo, Uganda receieves a constant replenishment of international aid, since 1987 donor countries and international financial institutions have invested heavily in Uganda it has therefore become imperative that the "Uganda model" succeed not only for the sake of their own credibility but also so that their investments are protected.

Rwanda too is a special case and has continued to enjoy the donations of the international donor community despite evidence of fraudulent practices. For example a World Bank official found that in 1999, that Belgium had registered $30 million in gold and gems from Rwanda and that there is no record of such exports in Kigali's official accounting (La Libre Beligique, 23-25 December, 2000).

Financing criminal activities of states, rather than financing agricultural development can only lead to consequences that are not only detrimental to the nationals of the countries involved but also excercabate ongoing international criminal activity. Although not conclusively proven, observers report that mining operations in areas under no state authority are used to launder receipts from arms and drug trafficking.

Given that 90 % of Africa's exports are agricultural products, agricultural growth has a major impact on poverty reduction. Agricultural growth can reduce consumer prices of non-tradable foods unless agricultural markets are heavily protected by the state, it can generate rural employment if government support in research, extension, infrastructure and marketing is extended to smallholders leading to jobs at a very low budget cost per job.

Many African countries have been unable to develop and implement an agricultural development strategy that generates growth and addressed rural poverty. Unlike Asian countries such as Taiwan, Thailand, Indonesia, Malysia and interestingly China that have made great strides in generating agricultural growth and reducing rural poverty. These countries reformed their large-scale ownership holdings into owner-operated family farms, with the exception of those growing plantation crops. These countries also invested heavily in agricultural technology for smallholders and refrained from subsidizing credit.

Could land reform support poverty reduction? The World Bank since the early to mid 1970s has been supportive of land reform and attempts were made to link lending programs to reforms in a number of countries including Zimbabwe. The World Development Report 1995 reaffirmed the World Bank's commitment to land reform. With the end of the Cold War, the fiscal unsustainability of large-scale commercial farm sectors and new approaches to land reform new opportunities may avail themselves in boosting agricultural growth and poverty reduction.

Many countries in the 1960s and 1970s were resistant to land reforms It therefore became difficult to target poverty reduction and rural development initiatives at smallholders. Nevertheless the Bank has financed many rural development projects and programmes including an integrated package of support to smallholder agricultural development for a specific area or region.

These projects some of which were called area development projects consisted of synergistic interventions in agricultural extension, research, marketing, input supply, credit, rural roads, water supply and electricity infrastructure and small scale irrigation. Sometimes the projects included a social component such as primary schools and health centres.

However many of these integrated rural development projects in the 1970s and 1980s were unsuccessful for the following reasons:

- Many governments were not committed to the projects and did not provide counterpart funding

- Inappropriate technology: although some projects included research components most failed to develop improved technologies that was appropriate to the beneficiaries

- These programmes were often designed in a top down manner without any input from the beneficiaries

- Lack of coordination at the local level: this emerged within government bureaucracies or parastatals which were often highly centralized.

The poor performance of integrated rural development projects led to the World Bank revising this approach for a more highly selective programme which entailed supporting sub-sector specific projects, each dealing with a specific component of rural development, such as agricultural extension, small-scale irrigation, rural roads, primary education and health care. It is clear that it has been possible to support a full array of interventions that are required for successful rural poverty reduction.

The question therefore is what elements of an agricultural and rural development and strategy should African countries employ to generate agricultural growth and reduce rural poverty. There is currently a broad consensus among agricultural and development professionals that the following key policy elements are fundamental to achieving agricultural and rural development as well as reducing poverty:

- There is a need to incorporate women farmers and workers in programme design and strategy

- There is also a need for substantial investments in economic and social infrastructure; for instance in health, education and nutrition in the rural areas

- Technology: It is essential that appropriate technology is developed for agricultural growth, this entails both private sector involvement and government financing of agricultural research in smallholder crops which are the basis for policy demands (see chapter on policy demands), sustainable systems and techniques, etc

- Land reform is required in countries where land is unequally distributed. Centralised ministries or parastatals are not good at implementing land reforms

- Strategies that promote an open economy and small farmer orientation is both economically efficient and most likely to reduce rural and urban poverty

- The foreign exchange, trade and taxation regime should not unfairly impede agricultural growth and favour the urban economy

RECOMMENDATIONS

Agricultural sector policies lie at the heart of development and poverty reduction initiatives in East Africa and consequently to be effective the following issues must be addressed:

1. Rural Focus: This requires the creation of new rural institutions to encourage all peasants to participate in agricultural activities. Appropriate backward and forward linkages must be forged between these rural institutions and the economy at large especially industry.

These rural institutions must be geared to enhancing rural participation in agriculture. Poor participatory practice can be found in poor institutional and individual understanding of the power paradigms at the local level. For an appropriate agricultural policy to be designed it is important that an appropriate form of rural participation is considered within the local socio-political context and in relation to the sort of agricultural outputs envisaged.

2. The Political Arena: New political institutions need to be shaped to ensure the effective participation in government at all levels of those classes which would benefit from rural development. Appropriate channels of communication and feedback should be shaped to enable these groups to take part in critical decisions relating to reallocation of resources.

The political focus on capital-centred development in the 1960s, resulted in a passive role for the majority of people whose participation was important in terms of local knowledge and labour. The emphasis was on the value of technological professional skills. The then narrow view of political participation saw participatory political culture only emerging as it grew out of economic and social development (Cohen and Uphoff, 1980).

This was then followed by the notion of people's participation in development. This people participation in rural agriculture and development has got to be linked with new political institutions related to civil liberties, growth, competition, policy stability, governance, conditionality, civil society, governments and policy formation

3. Government Machinery: Inherited colonial sets of government ministries and structures of government administrations need to be redesigned so that it is capable of addressing policy demands of rural agriculture. For example the RNF sector is not adequately addressed under inherited government ministries as it neither belongs within the domain of agricultural ministries nor to industry ministries.

4. A Long-Term Physical Plan: e g 20 years should be formulated to create balanced industrial and agricultural sectors to increase productive employment opportunities and raise living standards in the countryside while reducing external dependence. This does not imply that the economy should no longer produce exports. Rather the export sector should be increasingly characterised by the production of more value added products in place of low cost raw materials.

The 1980 Lagos plan of Action for Africa's development is such a plan prepared for the OAU. In response to the declining world prices of African exports. A long-term physical plan should envisage bringing the commodities issue back on the international agenda and through a supply management regime, bring some medium-term balance into the commodity market.

International efforts to stabilise and strengthen commodity markets have come virtually to a halt, most of the existing commodity agreements have collapsed. The huge losses sustained by most commodity exporting countries have accounted for much of the growth in their foreign debts

The agricultural commodities situation is critical to African agricultural policy. The logic of the present situation points to the need for some supply management. But the supply management needed now would have to be different from the short-term supply management efforts carried out through the international commodity agreements under UNCTAD's Integrated Programme for Commodities (IPC). It is imperative to contemplate management of supply over a longer-term combined with diversification away from production of commodities in persistent surplus.

If need be Africa would have to organise this longer-term supply management by themselves under the auspices of Africa's Priority Programme for Economic Recovery (APPER) which was adopted by the UN General Assembly, as the

United Nations Programme of Action for African Economic Recovery and Development (UNPAAERD).

However such an approach should not be regarded as a confrontation with the developed countries, but as a means of giving much-needed stability and strength to world commodity markets in the interest of both producing and consuming countries. Positive action on the commodity issue is a fundamental factor affecting agricultural policy and economic growth initiatives; in this regard therefore:

> cocoa and coffee exporting countries of Africa should give full support to the supply management schemes of these 2 commodity bodies, while for other commodities in medium term oversupply Africa should consider the development of their own supply management schemes.

> countries in adverse economic situations however should be exempt from having to cut the volume of their exports as per the supply management schemes, so long as their exports remain as less than a small proportion of the value of exports of the commodity from all members of the scheme.

All in all the future of agricultural policy in Africa will be based on the primacy of institutions (rural institutions in particular). Most definitions of institutions "have in common the general idea of an institution as the locus of a regularised or crystallised principle of conduct, action or behaviour that governs a crucial area of social life and that endures over time" (Martinussen, 1990)

In the 1980s development problems were seen to arise from too much state and too little civil society. One leading critic of state intervention Douglass North (Nobel Prize, economics winner, 1993) argued that some specific institutions inhibit development and lead to large transaction costs. But North also took the view that institutions were not necessarily disturbing to the functioning of markets. They formed, rather, an integral part of the development of markets. Institutions reflected the "rules, enforcement characteristics of rules, and norms of behaviour that structure repeated human interaction" (North 1989) this includes the duties in economic transactions and the political process. In other words, institutions represent the formalised rules of interaction in a society.

Consequently agricultural policy should encompass major institutional approaches to the problems of rural development. Transaction costs are high in LDCs, the more complex the transactions the higher the costs hence the need for appropriate institutional arrangements. Authorities such as North claim that

institutions point to the way societies develop and constitute the key to an understanding of historical change. Rural institutions represent the culture that provides the key to development. Agricultural policy must incorporate the policy
demands of the culture e.g. nomadic pastoralism in Somalia.

However, appropriate agricultural policy can only come about if development-
promoting forms of government, institutions and organisations exist. (Which can
reduce transaction costs) In this regard the World Bank has recognised that much
of the failure of SAPs was due to a "crisis of governance". The World Bank 1997
World Development Report "The State in a Changing World" put forward ideas
about how to promote good government, it is no longer a matter of only "getting
the prices right" but also the rural institutions. This report reflected the way forward to Agricultural policy analysis, in recognising the growing need for proper
institutions in structurally adjusted countries in Africa

BIBLIOGRAPHY

Gibbon, Peter	A Political Economy of the World Bank, 1970–1990	Paper delivered to the Council for the Development of Economic and Social Research in Africa, 9-12 Sep. 1991, Dakar
Easton, David	A Framework for Political Analysis	(1965) Prentice Hall, New York
Easton, David	The Political System	(1953) A.Knopf, New York
McMaster, D.N.	Speculations on the Coming of the Banana to Baganda	(1963) Uganda Journal, 27:2
Wrigley, C.C.	Buganda:An Outline	(1957) Economic History Review, Series 2, 10, London
World Bank	Sub-Saharan Africa: From Crisis to Sustainable Growth, A Long Term Perspective Study	(1989) World Bank, Washington D.C.
World Bank	Accelerated Development in Sub-Saharan Africa:An Agenda for Action	(1981) World Bank, Washington D.C.
World Bank	Annual World Development Report	(1989) Oxford University Press, Oxford
Republic of Kenya	Sessional Paper No. 4 of 1981 on National Food Policy	(1981) Government Printers, Nairobi
Watts, Michael	Peasants Under Contract in Bernstein, Henry et al., The Food Question: Profit versus People	(1990) Earthscan Publications, London
World Bank	Uganda: The Challenge of Growth and Poverty Reduction	1995, World Bank, Washington D.C.

Parsons, D.	Agriculture in Uganda	(1970) Oxford University Press, Oxford
Lockheed, M, Jamison, D., Lau, L.	Farmer Education and Farm Efficiency—a Survey	(1980)
Mbilingi, M., Mbughuni, P. (eds.)	Education in Tanzania with a Gender Perspective	(1991) SIDA, Stockholm
Livingstone, Ian	Development Economics and Policy	(1981) George Allen & Unwin, London
Johnson, B.F.	Studies in Agricultural Economics, Trade & Development, Vol. II, no. 1	(1972) Food Research Institute, London
MPED	Manpower and Employment in Uganda, National Manpower Survey	(1989) MPED, Kampala
Twinomujuni, G.	Capital Goods Industry in Uganda: A Focus on Small Scale Industry	(1992) MA Dissertation, Makerere University, Kampala
Schatzberg, Michael, G.	The Political Economy of Kenya	(1987) Praeger, London
Farzin, Hossein	Food Aid: Positive and Negative Effects in Somalia:	(1991) The Journal of Developing Areas, Dakar
African Rights	Land Tenure, the Creation of Famine and Prospects for Peace in Somalia, Discussion Paper No. 1	(Oct. 1993) African Rights, London
African Rights	Somalia: Operation Restore Hope: A Preliminary Assessment	(May 1993) African Rights, London
Inspectie Ontwikkelingssamenwerking Velde	Humanitarian Aid to Somalia	1994, IOV, Amsterdam
Lofchie, Michael F., et al.	Africa's Agrarian Crisis: the Roots of Famine	(1986) Lynne Rienner Publishers Inc., New York
World Bank	Coping with External Debt in the 1980s	(1985) World Bank, Washington D.C.

Roemer, Michael	Economic Development in Africa: Performance since Independence and a Strategy for the Future	(1982) in Daedalus, p.132, London
Palmer, Robert & Parsons, Neil (Eds.)	The Roots of Rural Poverty in Central and Southern Africa	(1977) Heinemann Educational Books, Ltd. London
UNECA	African Alternative to SAPs: A Framework for Transformation and Recovery	(1989) UNECA, Addis Ababa
World Bank	Adjustment in Africa: Reforms, Results and the Road Ahead	(1994) World Bank, Oxford
Adedeji, Adebayo (Ed.)	Africa Within the World: Beyond Dispossession and Dependence	(1993) Zed Books, London
Lewis, W.A.	Economic Development with Unlimited Supplies of Labour	(1954) Manchester School 22, p.139-91, Manchester
Lewis, W.A.	The Theory of Economic Growth	(1955) Allen & Unwin, London
Picket, J. Singer H. (Eds.)	Towards Economic Recovery in Sub-Saharan Africa	(1990) Routledge, London
United Nations Secretary General's Export Group on Africa's Commodity Problems	Africa's Commodity Problems: Towards a Solution	(1990) United Nations, Geneva
Cohen, J.M., Uphoff, N.T.	Participants Place in Rural Development: Seeking Clarity Through Specificity	(1980) World Development, Vol. 8, pp 213-235, London
Martinussen, John	General Introduction to the Theme in the Context of Development Studies in Selected Approaches to the Study of Institutions in Development	(1990) Occasional Paper no. 1, International Development Studies, Roskilde University, Roskilde
North Douglass C.	Institutions and Economic Growth: A Historical Introduction	(1989) in World Development Vol. 17, No. 9, New York

World Bank	World Development Report, 1997: the State in a Changing World	(1997) Oxford University Press, Oxford
World Bank	Poverty and Hunger: Issues and Options for Food Security in Developing Countries	(1986) World Bank, Washington DC
World Bank	The Challenge of Growth and Poverty Reduction. A World Bank Country Study	(1996) World Bank Washington DC
World Bank	African Development Indicators	(2000) World Bank Washington DC
Hakim, C.	Secondary Analysis in Social Research	(1982) Allen & Unwin, London
Downing, T.,	"Assessing Socio-Economic Vulnerability to Famine: Frameworks, Concepts & Applications"	Final Report to the USAID Famine Early Warning System Project (1990) Washington
FAO	"World Food Security Compact"	(1983) FAO
Sen, A.,	Poverty and Famines	(1981) Oxford: Claredon Press
Pearson L.B., (Chairman)	Report of the Commission on International Development: Partners in Development	(1970) Praeger, New York
Mehmet, Oxay	"Effectiveness of Foreign Aid: The Case of Somalia", Journal of Modern African Studies, 9 (1)	(1971), May, Oxford
Bhagwati J.,	"The Tying of Aid": Progress Report, TD (7) Supp. 4 UN	(1967) UNCTAD Secretariat
World Bank,	Accelerated Development in Sub-Saharan Africa: An Agenda for Action	(1981) Washington D.C.
World Bank,	Sub-Saharan Africa: Progress Report on Development Prospects and Programs	(1983) Washington D.C.

UNECA,   Critical Analysis of the Coun-   (1982) Addis Ababa
          try Presentations of African
          Least Developed Countries in
          the Light of the Lagos Plan of
          Action and the Final Act of
          Lagos

Gourevitch P.,   "Letter from the Congo" The   (1997) New York
                  New Yorker, 4 Aug

Jayne, T.S.   Agricultural policy reform and   Aug 10-16 (1997) California
               productivity change in Africa.
               Paper presented at the XXIII
               International Conference of
               Agricultural Economists,
               Sacremento

Jones, S   Food Market Reform: The   (1995) Food Policy, Oxford
            changing role of the State

Jones, S and Wickrema,   The Use of Conditionality in   (1998), Oxford Policy Man-
                          Reform: Food Markets in   agementOxford, UK
                          Africa. Policy Briefing Note 1

Binswanger, Hans P. and   "The World Bank's Strategy for   (1996) World Bank, Washing-
Pierre Landell-Mills   Reducing Poverty and Hun-   ton DC
                           ger: A Report to the Develop-
                           ment Community",
                           Environmentally Sustainable
                           Development Studies and
                           Monographs Series No.4

http://www.worldbank.org

http://www.IMF.org

http://www.FAO.org

http://www.BBC.co.uk

http://www.IDS.ac.uk